The Humane City

Perth, Australia

But he was also an optimist. He knew that the signs in the sky of this city were made only from gas and glass. He knew gas and glass could be broken, the gas set free, the glass bent into other shapes and that even the city itself was something imagined by men and women, and if it could be imagined into one form, it could be imagined into another.

Peter Carey
Illywhacker

The Humane City
Cities as if People Matter

John R. Short

Basil Blackwell

First published 1989

Basil Blackwell Ltd
108 Cowley Road, Oxford, OX4 1JF, UK

Basil Blackwell Inc.
432 Park Avenue South, Suite 1503
New York, NY 10016, USA

British Library Cataloguing in Publication Data

Short, John R. (John Rennie), 1951–
   The humane city: cities as if people matter
   1. Western world. Urban regions. Human
   geographical features
   I. Title
   307.7'6'091821   OCLC 18463 935
   ISBN 0–631–15823–5
   ISBN 0–631–15824–3   Pbk

Library of Congress Cataloging in Publication Data

Short, John R.
      The humane city: cities as if people matter/John R. Short.
         p.   cm.
      Bibliography: p.
      Includes index.
      ISBN 0–631–15823 5
      ISBN 0–631–15824–3 (pbk.)
      1. Cities and towns. I. Title.
   HT161.S476 1989
   307.7'8–dc19   88–8125

Typeset in 11/13 pt Sabon
by Graphicraft Typesetters Ltd., Hong Kong.
Printed in Great Britain by TJ Press (Padstow) Ltd, Cornwall

For

David Cadman, Jack Mundey and Toni Tulla

Contents

Acknowledgements

The idea for the book first arose from my meeting David Cadman. Since 1980 we have had a series of discussions in Reading, Cambridge, London and Suffolk on the topic of places 'as if people mattered'. He introduced me to a whole range of 'alternative' literature. We should have written the book together but pressures of time and factors of distance precluded a collaborative venture. Chapter 2 is a much revised version of unpublished papers that we wrote together. The spirit of the book owes much to David.

I also have more specific debts. Chapter 6 benefited from discussions with Steven Buckle of the Philosophy Department, Australian National University. Chapter 7 is an amended version of an invited contribution to a *Festschrift* for Roy Mellor of Aberdeen University; Chris Maher gave the invitation for the lecture that forms the basis for Appendix 1, and Appendix 3 arose from an invitation secured through Pat Troy.

Rob Freestone read through one version of the manuscript and Ian Winter read through two. Only good friends could have made so many criticisms. Pat Troy and Clem Lloyd read other versions and made suggestions. Katalin Kuszko in Canberra had the difficult job of typing the manuscripts of a book which went through six versions, a job she performed with skill and patience. The 'definitely-the-last' drafts were completed in Reading by Chris Holland. Chris has typed most of my work. Her skill, humour and technical ability are very much appreciated.

The book was completed in Reading but the bulk of the text was written during my stay at the Urban Research Unit of the Australian National University. I was given a two-year Senior Research Fellowship in 1985. The conditions were ideal for quiet thinking and slow writing. I am indebted to the general atmosphere created by Katalin Kuszko, Rob Freestone, Chris Paris, Hal Kendig, Max Neutze, Pat Troy, Ian Winter, Liz Cocke, Susan Faulbaum, Peter Allen, Roger Jones, Will Sanders, Peter Self and Jill Walker.

Writing is a way of examining society but it can also become a way of avoiding life. All writers know when to start writing, few know when to stop. Adrienne made me understand when to put down the pen. And why.

1 Introduction

There are times which are not ordinary, and in such times it is not enough to follow the road. It is necessary to know where it leads, and, if it leads nowhere to follow another. The search for another involves reflection, which is uncongenial to the bustling people who describe themselves as practical, because they take things as they are and leave them as they are. But the practical thing for the traveller who is uncertain of his past is not to proceed with the utmost rapidity in the wrong direction: it is to consider how to find the right one.

R. H. Tawney
The Acquisitive Society

Cities should be places where ordinary citizens can lead dignified and creative lives. Why this is not the case and how we can achieve this goal are the subjects of this book. Part I considers some of the reasons why, and Part II looks at some of the ways how.

This is not a long book, but these are busy times. The three appendices are summaries of the general arguments for both broad and specific audiences; although they are at the end of the book, you would benefit from reading them first.

Some readers of the manuscript identified two main weaknesses; the idealism of the text and its optimism. I plead guilty on both counts. Let me elaborate. My 'idealism' is not dependent on a model of humanity lacking self-interest. We may agree with David Hume that 'every man ought to be supposed a knave and to have no other end than private interest'. However, we are also members of a society as much as we are individuals. In one of the most interesting books of recent years Robert Axelrod (1984) has shown that it is in people's own interests to pursue courses of mutual cooperation. I enjoyed his book because it gives formal proofs and cerebral legitimation for my gut feeling. Self-interest has been given ideological pride of place, an understandable reading given the moral codification of capitalism, but Axelrod reminds us of our social selves, and our capacity and our need for cooperation.

The 'optimism' of the book derives from my failure to examine those power relations which mitigate against emancipatory change. In Part I, for example, the exposition moves from a description of the present to an indication of a possible future with scant regard for the problems involved. This is deliberate. I want to concentrate attention on the constraints on our imagination rather than the social and political barriers to change. The most subtle power relations are internalized in our thinking; they do not allow us to see alternatives to the status quo and so impoverish our imagination that we are blind to the existence of other possible worlds. Formal relations of power are buttressed by such ideas, accepted 'facts' and initial assumptions. This book is an exercise in mapping out a different ideological terrain.

A city, in a capitalist society, is a complex place. It is, at one and the same time, an expression of architectural design, home to various social and ethnic groups, the scene of much business activity, the responsibility of various central and local governments. And much else. These various activities have provided the basis for a whole series of languages of and for the city. However, the languages of powerful groups, especially the calculus of business and the associated designs of government, do more than just describe one aspect of urban reality; they set the agenda for public discussion. Definitions of what makes a good city have been dominated by questions of economic growth and issues of administrative convenience. In this book I want to outline the vocabulary for cities as if people matter. We need first to discuss those languages in which the rich diversity of human needs are ignored, simplified or suppressed; discourses that treat the city as if people do not matter. This is the subject of Part I. In Part II I seek to demonstrate why the empowerment and engagement of ordinary citizens should be our main goals, and what sort of problems may arise in the process. My starting-point is to see citizens as the solution to, not the cause of, urban problems.

The term 'cities' is used in a classical rather than statistical

Plate 1.1 Cities are complex places. The range of activities is hinted at in this view of Sydney.

manner; it is used to cover the range of concentrations of people, from small towns to metropolitan regions. By focusing on cities I do not seek to exclude country-dwellers. Rather I am focusing attention on those more communal places enlivened with regular human action and contact.

The material is almost entirely based on cities in advanced capitalist countries. My silence on the experience of the vast majority of the world's population who are concentrated in large cities in poor countries reflects a lack of knowledge rather than a lack of concern. Urban 'solutions' from the rich world have been exported to the poor world, with, more often than not, deleterious consequences. I think the time and circumstances are ripe for a reversal of the flow. We have much to learn from the self-help schemes of the city-dwellers in the Third World cities with their organizational mechanisms for coping with few formal jobs and limited public services. For the moment, however, I have restricted my comments to the urban experience with which I am most familiar.

The mere reiteration of the phrase 'cities as if people matter' will not get us very far. The humanistic perspective is not in itself a solution or an end-point of explanations, but a starting position for those seeking sustainable, liveable solutions to our social malaise. And there is malaise, whether it be experienced in communal revolt, random acts of violence, anonymous bouts of depression or agonizing loneliness. Some of our ills are not new. People have always been depressed, and street violence is not simply a product of the twentieth century. Where we are in time is not so much the problem – more a source of emancipation. We now have more resources, knowledge and abilities at our collective disposal than ever before. It seems such a waste not to use the opportunities presented to us by our position in history and our location in society to build better societies and to create more humane cities.

In looking at cities even from radical perspectives, we are weighed down by the past. The historical legacy takes many forms. There is the physical presence of buildings designed and constructed for uses past and sometimes forgotten. The erosion of history has left us the palaces, the courts and the mansions; the profane and the ordinary have usually long gone. This differential weathering has led to the glorification of the past and to the downgrading of the present. There is an important element in contemporary thought which stresses the ugliness and the alienation of the built environment. This easy denigration of the modern city can lead to an intellectual suburbanization, a withdrawal from the essential concerns of the majority of people who live in cities. Social solutions, as opposed to private retreats, require a renewed concern with the city and its citizens.

The potential for creating new places is limited by the existing physical infrastructure of utilities and services and the mosaic of human communities. The pattern of roads and sewers, and other lines of supply, together with the sheer mass and durability of the present stock of domestic and commercial buildings, constitute major physical constraints to change, while the infinitely subtle network of human communities can be destroyed more easily than it can be created. Proposals that require the large-

Plate 1.2 Differential weathering has left us the palaces and mansions.
Cliveden, Buckinghamshire (*above*), and Blickling Hall, Norfolk
(*below*), both in the UK, stand as symbols of former economic and
political power.

scale destruction of existing places, or which ignore the primacy of human relationships, should thus be regarded with deep scepticism.

The examination of society is difficult. Society is experienced as well as studied, something to be involved in, yet something to describe; a drama in which we are both actors and audience. The tension is obvious in this text. All academic authors have a personal voice lurking behind their prose; most of the time it is kept in check by the use of the 'it can be suggested' kind of phrase and the studious avoidance of the 'I believe' type of opening statement. This voice keeps intruding in this text because it is part descriptive, part prescriptive, as much polemical as analytical.

The tenor of the book arose from the dissatisfaction I felt with much academic writing on the city, including my own. Two major positions exist: first, there are the radicals. Over the past ten to twenty years great effort has been concerned with showing how the forces of capital have determined urban outcomes. We now know that decision-making is structured and that capital is an important force in the shaping of cities and the lives of citizens. Continual reiteration of these ideas has led to the growing irrelevance of much academic analysis: such armchair theorizing is now merely radical posturing that lacks substance, conviction or any real point of contact with political forces. To hear these academic debates is to listen to the stale voices of despair. Second, there are the 'new realists', those academics who mindlessly repeat the words and message of the free-marketeers. In an attempt to be 'relevant', 'up to date' and 'hard', they see solutions only in terms of attracting capital and making the city attractive for capital investors. Of the two positions, then, one is a position of naive radicalism, the other of private market brutalism. We can, I believe, see the city as something other than 'marxopolis' or 'profitopolis', and citizens as more than just puppets of old political theories or new market forces.

In this book I have sought to see people as the subjects as well as the objects of history. If we refuse the easy option of waiting for the Great Day when revolution comes and everything will be better, and if we accept the possibility of emancipatory human action here and now, with all the compromises involved, then we have an important duty to join in the debate over the means and ends of such action. This book is my contribution to that discussion which refuses to accept the inevitability of revolution or the continual hegemony of capital. I have done no more than provide provisional notes. I do not wish to provide a blueprint for the construction of cities. There seems little point in criticizing rigid, top-down, approaches and then presenting a fully-fashioned design manual. My aim is to find ways of enabling people to make their own liveable cities and truly human places.

There are two sorts of academic book. The largest category is the 'full-stop' variety, those that seek to end a debate. I have covered this area so thoroughly, is the unwritten message, that nothing more of value can be said. Then there are the 'question-mark' type, which try to open up lines for further discussion and seek (explicitly) to raise more questions than they provide answers to. This book is of the second type.

On re-reading the manuscript for the final time, I have to admit to a feeling of disappointment. I know (hope?) that this is the natural reaction of an author to a completed work: the literary equivalent of postnatal depression. But there is something else to which I have to admit: re-reading made me realize how much has escaped me. The book is an introduction in a double sense: it refers only briefly to a wide body of written work and a broad scope of human practice; moreover, I cannot claim to have fully satisfied my initial expectations for the book. Between the promise and the reality is the gap which separates our dreams from our lives.

Part I
Cities as if People Don't Matter

The ideas of the ruling class are, in every age, the ruling ideas: the class which is the dominant material force in society is at the same time its dominant intellectual force.

Karl Marx and Frederick Engels
The German Ideology

In this section I will consider three major forces which can lead to cities as if people don't matter: the power of capital to create the city simply as a revenue-generating machine; the power of professionals to create cities in their own image; and the power of existing political structures to marginalize many citizens. These forces cannot be overestimated, but I don't want to present just a tale of woe. Each of the three chapters also presents ways of harnessing these forces to more progressive ends. Social forces present us with opportunities as well as constraints.

2 Cities as if Only Capital Matters

Our first impression must surely be the degree to which the individual city appears to have been not so much planned for human purposes as simply beaten into some sort of shape by repeated strokes from gigantic hammers — the hammer of technology and applied power, the overwhelming drive of national self interest, the single-minded pursuit of economic gain.

Barbara Ward
Home of Man

Capitalist societies are so called because of the power of capital, a power which affects the basic economic structure of cities as well as the rhythms of everyday urban life. It is a power which constrains but is not total. There are still opportunities for progressive change, spaces where more life-enhancing cultures cluster and cling. In this chapter I will consider the power and examine some of the spaces.

The Cities of Economic Man*

In the early part of the eighteenth century, most countries were predominantly agricultural societies. The population was scattered throughout the country in farms, villages and small towns, largely dependent upon human and animal power and the energy of wood, water and wind. Such manufacturing as existed, was

---

* In this context the term 'man' is not used to mean people. The sexist language reflects the sexist practice.

Plate 2.1   The Carron Company first started iron-working in the eighteenth century. This factory, near Falkirk in Scotland, closed in 1983 – from industrial to post-industrial in two hundred years.

mainly, though not exclusively, the work of craftsmen, and markets were places at which people exchanged or traded goods on a personal basis.

As the cradle of the Industrial Revolution, Britain provided the earliest example of the changes to come. Here capitalist industrialism, with its new machines and new forms of power based on coal and steam, had a marked effect on the places where people lived and worked. From the late eighteenth and throughout the nineteenth centuries increasing numbers of men, women and children were both pushed off the land and drawn away from the farms and country areas into the industrial towns, cities and ports. By the middle of the nineteenth century the rural–urban balance had firmly swung in favour of the urban centres. The countryside may have been bleak for the labouring classes but the cities were no better. The Industrial Revolution created cities dominated by private greed often at the expense of broader social values, community concerns and human dignity. The following extracts from Engels's *The Conditions of the Working Class in England*, written in 1884–5, provide only one illustration of the conditions.

> ... after visiting the slums of the metropolis, one realised for the first time that these Londoners have been forced to sacrifice the best qualities of their human nature, to bring to pass all the marvels of civilisation which crowd their city; that a hundred powers which slumbered within them have remained inactive, have been suppressed in order that a few might be developed more fully and multiply through union with those of others.

> . . . . .

> In the lower lodging-houses, ten, twelve, sometimes twenty persons of both sexes, all ages and various degrees of nakedness, sleep indiscriminately huddled together upon the floor. These dwellings are usually so damp, filthy, and ruinous, that no one could wish to keep his horse in one of them.

The rise of capitalist industrialism involved the development of a capitalist ideology, which extolled the virtues of the division of labour and the efficiency of the 'invisible hand' of perfect competition and self-interest. The market was likened to a finely balanced mechanism, and the individual worker was seen as a cog in the machine of production performing a specialized but anonymous task. In time, specialism, competition and the measurement of merit by price, became not a description of the way in which markets might behave under 'perfect' conditions but the intellectual foundations of a 'natural' order of things, a belief, almost a creed, which held that competitive, selfish behaviour brought about the greatest good for all.

To be sure, the dominant ideas did not go unchallenged. Throughout the eighteenth and nineteenth centuries different models of society were espoused by social commentators as varied as Tom Paine, William Morris, Peter Kropotkin and Karl Marx. Their ideas were taken up by various utopian, anarchist and socialist groups. The alternative theorists and opposition groups challenged the rule of capital and in their actions put limits on capitalist forms of development. The industrial cities of the nineteenth century were also places were labour organizations flourished, self-help schemes such as building societies were established and communities banded together to resist the worst excesses of a rampant capitalism. Eventually legislation was enacted that improved urban conditions, partly through the influence of social critics, partly through the fear of social unrest. The worst excesses were tempered but the market system continued, with its commitment to competition, production and growth.

The Cities of Mass Consumption

The twentieth century, and particularly the period from the end of the Second World War, has seen the transformation of capitalist economies. In the richer countries, rising standards of living have been obtained for the mass of the population. Inequalities in wealth and disparities in life chances persist, but social conflict has been reduced by high-performance economies.

During this period large-scale production and mass consumption became commonplace. The emphasis was on the volume and the continuity of consumption, providing the stimulus for planned obsolescence and the creation of waste. Vance Packard describes a place which takes these trends to their logical conclusion:

> In Cornucopia City, as I understand it, all the buildings will be made of a special paper-mache. These houses can be torn down and rebuilt every spring and fall at house cleaning time. The motor cars of Cornucopia will be made of a light weight plastic that develops fatigue and begins to melt if driven more than 4,000 miles. Owners return in their old motor cars at the regular turn in date ... And a special additional bond will be awarded to those families able to turn in four or more motor cars at each disposal date.
>
> One fourth of the factories in Cornucopia City will be located on the edge of a cliff, and the ends of their assembly lines can be swung to the front or rear doors depending upon the public demand for the product being produced. When demand is slack, the end of the assembly line will be swung to the rear door and output of refrigerators or other products will drop out of sight and go directly to their graveyards without first overwhelming the consumer market. (Packard, 1961, 15–16)

The production of waste entailed the creation of needs. In order to ensure production it became necessary to maintain demand. A great deal of time and effort was now spent telling people that the things they needed were not the things they had. It was the pursuit of the unattainable.

The emphasis on consumption was apparent not only in determining an individual's social status but also in national identity. Thus the great American dream or the Australian way of life was not a description of the quality of social relations but a pride in the scale of conspicuous consumption.

In *The Affluent Society* (1958), Kenneth Galbraith made the point that the conventional wisdom in the USA was still dominated by dismal economics doctrines. Ideas fashioned in bleaker times continued to prevail, affecting US governmental attitudes to unemployment, poverty and public investment projects. This bedrock of economic pessimism has surfaced in Reaganomics and Thatcherism. Their policies of economic monetarism and social Darwinism hark back to pre-affluence times and reference the gloominess of older economic doctrines.

There have been critical reactions to the age of affluence. The environmental movement, for example, was reawakened in the 1960s as the image of an increasingly polluted world took hold in the popular imagination. Environmental romanticism was combined with ecological analysis to pose an alternative view of the relationship between people and environment, and in the 1980s we can see the maturing of this culture in various ways, from elements of the peace movement and the women's movement, down to the more mundane opening of health-food restaurants. The age of growth has produced the no-growth movement.

The age of mass consumption is thus a time of competing sets of ideas, with the most prevailing sets stressing growth and disposability. Its urban effects are encapsulated in the two solid metaphors of our time – the suburb and the motor car.

The suburb is neither country nor town. It is the symbol of separatism between home and work, a place for child-rearing and -launching; for fathers a place of retreat, for mothers a place of work, and for parents the sign of sacrifice. It is a statement of intent, a marker on the route of social mobility, a starting-point and a destination. Lewis Mumford characterizes it thus:

Plate 2.2   An American dream?

> A multitude of uniform unidentifiable houses, lined up inflexibly
> at uniform distances, on uniform roads, in a treeless communal
> waste, inhabited by people of the same class, same income, the
> same age group, witnessing the same television performances,
> eating the same tasteless prefabricated foods, from the same freez-
> ers, conforming in every outward and inward respect to a com-
> mon mould, manufactured in the central metropolis ... a low
> grade uniform environment from which escape is impossible ...
> an asylum for the preservation of illusion. (1961, 553–63)

Much criticism of the suburbs comes from the arch superiority of
commentators such as Mumford eager to distance themselves
from the mass of low- to middle-income groups. Many suburbs
have vitality despite the segregation between home and workplace. Despite the suburban tendency to turn households in on
themselves, communities have developed and flourished. Despite
the unfair gender division of labour, for many people the suburban house and garden provides the only avenue of creativity in
their lives. Blanket dismissals of suburbia are too easy and too

wrong; we need to enhance the individual freedoms they provide, opening them up to a wider range of ethnic and social groups.

The motor car is the symbol of the twentieth century, capturing the ambivalence of the era. On the one hand, its production has provided highly paid jobs and its consumption has bestowed a measure of mobility. On the other hand, its mass production techniques have brought the alienating work experience of the conveyor-belt and its use has placed restrictions on pedestrians and other road-users. Cars clog up our cities, assaulting our basic senses and transforming built environments into dangerous, smelly, noisy places. At concentrated points people are relegated to small pavements and narrow walkways or ignored altogether. These are places as if only cars mattered.

The use of the car and the development of the suburb are most evident in that symbolic city of the twentieth century, Los Angeles. Here is autopia, a hundred suburbs in search of a city: 'an endless plain endlessly gridded with endless streets, peppered endlessly with ticky-tacky houses clustered in indistinguishable neighbourhoods, slashed across by endless freeways that have destroyed any community spirit that may once have existed' (Banham, 1971, 161). For the urban snobs, LA is there to be rubbished; 'a big hard-boiled city with about as much personality as a throwaway paper cup' according to Philip Marlowe. The comments tell us as much about the commentators as the city. With its vast suburbs and miles of freeways carrying seemingly endless traffic, LA is the city of the post-industrial world, a place of excitement and variety, with some of the best and much of the worst of our contemporary society. It is the city of mass consumption, as redolent of an age as Florence is of the Renaissance. To comment on LA is to reveal your prejudices about the urbanism of modernity.

The Contemporary Capitalist City

Capitalism is a system in continual flux. There are two basic types of capital movement, each with its own urban impact: long waves and the shorter phases of investment switching.

Plate 2.3   Los Angeles, the city of mass consumption, its suburbs an icon of modernism.

Capitalist development has, historically, taken not a linear path but one in which booms are followed by slumps. Kondratieff cycles (named after a Soviet economist) of approximately fifty years have been recorded. In these long waves, boom periods are characterized by the adoption of inventions, the development of new production processes and the consumption of a whole series of new goods. The fifty-year cycles involve a complete restructuring of economies, such as the iron and steel phase of the late nineteenth century, the consumer goods phase in the post-1945 period or the more recent growth of high technology and bio-chemical industries. Each wave produces a unique built form from the Coketowns of the nineteenth-century iron and steel era to the small towns of the 1980s which are now attracting computer firms and biochemical research establishments, and the consequent development of sets of skills held by particular groups in particular cities. New waves make redundant both the skills and the cities forged during previous waves. The contemporary decline of industrial urban Britain or smokestack America, and the weakened power of industrial unions in both countries, mark the end of one wave and the beginning of a new one.

The shorter term switching of investment is also a basic feature of capitalism. The search for higher profits has always been the dynamic of capitalism but since the Second World War a number of significant trends have increased the amount and speed of this switching. There has been an increasing concentration of economic activity: the ten largest firms in most sectors account for over 90 per cent of production. These modern corporations are multinational, multiproduct enterprises, which find it relatively easy to switch investment from low-profit to high-profit sectors, move production from high-labour-cost to low-labour-cost areas and concentrate advertising in growing consumer markets. These changes have marked redistributional consequences. Whole groups of workers can be made redundant and major cities can lose their economic *raison d'être*. The current scramble by capital away from declining sectors and cities may be rational for individual capitals but has enormous social costs for stranded workers and abandoned cities.

Coping with Capital

The major response of most local and central governments has been to attract footloose capital. Fiscal incentives, tax holidays, provision of cheap accommodation, grants and a host of other carrots have been dangled in front of capital. This strategy has some political appeal because it looks as if the authorities are doing something. Attracting capital may suit politicians with limited electoral horizons, and fire-up well-meaning groups wanting to do something here and now, but it does not provide long-term solutions. During a recession the amount of investment is limited; *your* gain is at *my* expense. If Newcastle gets the only car factory being built, then that is Liverpool's loss. By its nature capital constantly searches for high profits. Different areas can easily find themselves outbidding each other with more attractive packages to attract capital which can and will move again when relative profits dip. A new widget factory built today at public expense may be closed next year because cheaper workers are found elsewhere or there is no longer a market for plastic, teak-veneer widgets. Fashions come and go. To build an economy on meeting such fashions is to face an uncertain future where short-term changes in demand can wreak long-term havoc.

Even if an area is successful in attracting investment, the provision of high-cost (for governments), low-paid (for the workers) jobs is no great thing. The quality of many jobs created by foot-loose capital is low, with few training schemes or possibilities for advancement. Attracting capital that employs young people to pack supermarket shelves doesn't seem such a big deal. Rather than merely counting jobs we need to consider the quality of employment. We need to develop useful work that harnesses and stretches human creativity without disrupting the ecological balance or creating unstable economies. If the investment produces damage to the environment, distorts the local economy so that workers' futures are based on unstable market conditions and creates boring, repetitive employment, then the proposed solution becomes part of the problem.

We need to question the concept of economic growth based on attracting footloose capital and replace it with the notion of investment based on human capital. The cooperative ventures in Italy, the *consorzi*, provide examples of how investment can be used to enhance local abilities. All localities contain people who have specific skills and potential expertise. A people-based strategy would concern itself with the question of how capital could be used to enhance their skills, entrepreneurial potential, collective and individual abilities.

In the medium term, employment strategies should be based on developing people's skills rather than exploiting their labour power. A car-making firm, for example, has a range of people with varying degrees of engineering skill and work-based loyalty. If the firm closes down, rather than seek to attract just any investment, the human capital could be used to develop cooperative schemes, targeting expertise to specific markets. In the much longer term, the goal should be a form of export substitution.

Many economists argue that the answer lies in building local and national economies that are so dynamic and responsive that they remain buoyant because they are always meeting market needs, even if these needs are changing. In an ideal world every city should be successful, but the realities of life, the existence of fixed capital (physical, social and emotional), means that cities and people are rarely so responsive. This strategy is only relevant therefore for a minority of places. For the majority a move towards greater self-sufficiency is the best solution to providing long-term, sustainable work, which means a reappraisal of urban economies. Rather than building economies geared towards world markets we should be thinking of creating local markets, for example encouraging local food production on allotments and gardens, or helping factories that provide for local needs. Local authorities have a role to play in selective purchasing schemes that help business. Rather than buy desks for schools from national firms, why not employ local carpenters? A great deal can be done once we replace the ideology of national and international markets. If nations were to adopt sensitive and selective import taxes this would create the necessary stimulation to export substitution. National- and local-level agreements could be used to provide positive help to selected Third World countries and thus avoid trade wars hitting the poorest people.

'Local' does not mean 'parochial', with all its connotations of smugness. I can imagine local economies in the rich world establishing trading arrangements with local economies from the eastern bloc and the Third World for mutually beneficial trade agreements. Ties at this level have greater human control than anonymous transfers of aid. When we have genuine links with other parts of the world, lasting international understanding can be achieved involving transfer of goods, people and ideas. We can think locally and act globally.

Greater self-sufficiency provides the possibility of sustainable employment. Some cities initially will be better placed than others, some skills more suitable than others, but a move towards self-sufficiency would make local economies less dependent on a narrow range of goods and services. There may be a difficult transition period but the longer-term consequences would be a reduction in costly transportation and a cultivation of human ingenuity. Ultimately, capital would be for the use of people rather than people for capital.

Dealing with Finance

If William Blake's 'dark satanic mills' are a powerful symbol of
nineteenth-century capitalism, then its latest icons must be the
NatWest office tower in the City of London or the skyscrapers of
Wall Street. In the most recent period economic man has grown
into financial man.

As levels of production and consumption have risen, increasing
amounts of finance have been needed. Producers need extra funds
to ensure the increased scale of their operation while consumers
need finance to maintain consumption. Loans and credit keep
the system going, and this increasing dependence has inevitably
meant a shift of influence away from industry and commercial
markets towards financial markets.

The finance has come from investors. Since 1960, incomes
have increased and personal savings ratios have doubled. Either
voluntarily, or as a part of a contract of employment, individuals
have passed increasingly large proportions of their income to
financial institutions. In Britain, for example, the main recipients
have been the insurance companies, the pension funds and the
building societies. In 1984, they had assets of £70 billion and
were investing at a rate of just under £25 billion a year, almost
twice the amount of money spent by the British Government on
public education in the same year. People have come into increasing contact with the finance sector through taking out mortgages
or life assurance, or contributing to pension funds. There is
strong financial propaganda emanating from a number of sup-
portive journals and special newspaper supplements which tell us
that happiness and security can be found in secure investments.
Just as the 'virtues' of competition, production, growth and consumption became integrated into the general thinking of early
capitalist society, so now the particular and narrow 'virtues' of
finance and its definition and measurement of viability, are being
advocated and accepted to the point that they are now an influential way of seeing reality in mature capitalist societies. The
development of economic man saw the ascendency of exchange
value over use value. The growth of financial man has involved
the victory of investment value over exchange value.

By controlling the flow of investment funds and setting their
own narrowly defined standards of what is 'institutionally

Plate 2.4   Downtown Sydney, Australia, has the phallic symbols of all would-be virile financial centres.

acceptable', the financial institutions determine the when and where of investment and what can and cannot be built. 'Acceptable' places are favoured and become over-supplied, while places that are out of favour, such as the inner areas of declining cities, find it very difficult to secure funds for urban renewal. Houses are built to meet the approval of building societies, and industrial estates and office buildings are designed and developed to meet the criteria of pension funds and insurance companies. Their value as investments takes primacy over their social value. When the investment made becomes the guiding force the city is designed more for maximum returns than social living. The clearest example of the sacrifice for greater profit of a city's liveability is to be seen in the centres of the larger towns and cities. Here finance capital is supreme and its power is evidenced in the giant concrete and glass towers, the symbols of cities as if capital mattered. There are some beautiful city office blocks and a few clusters of buildings which mutually enhance one another, but

Plate 2.5 Private investment floods into favoured sectors such as office development in Reading, Berkshire (*above*), while inner-city areas in Glasgow, Scotland (*below*), find it difficult to attract investment.

these are the exceptions. The dominant pattern is of a myriad of architectural designs competing for sole aesthetic dominance and maximum rentals. The end result is a city centre designed more for profit than people. The centres of our greatest cities are rarely places to linger or enjoy; they have been given over to Mammon. The hearts of our cities have been sold to the highest bidders.

To create liveable cities we need to guide investment, so that profit is not bought at the expense of humanity. One way is to make the finance institutions set a certain appreciable amount of their holdings into a community fund. Areas identified as needing investment would then be given extra funds over and above normal government grants. Finance capital could then be used to help the most needy, and would thus have a positive redistributional quality rather than its usual regressive one of helping the rich to get richer.

The age of high mass consumption unwittingly gave power to the consumer. As individuals most of us are small purchasers, together we are a powerful force. In the 1960s and 1970s progressive forces began to organize consumer power. Consumer rights about the quality, labelling and quantity of products were established. Now, in the age of finance capital, most of us are investors. Individually, most of us still have little power, but banded together we can have an important influence. Along with consumers' associations we need associations of investors, which can raise issues about the quality, quantity and direction of investment.

A major problem lies in the system whereby anonymous investors leave their savings in the hands of institutions that have no responsibility other than maximizing investment. We need to encourage the concept of 'ethical' investment and the practice of 'local' investment. Ethical investment is capitalism with a human face, investors being aware of their own responsibility. The partly successful campaign against investment in South Africa is a case in point. As investors – and most of us are willing or unconscious investors in some way – we have a social responsibility to ensure not only high returns, but that our money is being used for the social good. We need a bill of conduct, a list of acceptable investments that provide both returns and wider benefits for citizens. Through local investment schemes we can specify that a certain percentage of our investment goes into acceptable local community projects. People may argue that this is irrational. But is the investment market so rational? Markets are just as fickle and are every bit as subject to fashion as any other human enterprise. Bank lending to Third World countries in the 1960s and 1970s is a case in point. At the time, the banks were eager to lend, but they now have the problem of huge defaults, while the Third World countries are suffering crippling debt repayments. The Third World debt is now around the incredible figure of $1,000 billion! So much for the rationality of finance capitalism.

We need to give more guidelines to the investing institutions; and we can do this without compromising our savings or financial security. In association with an export substitution programme city region investment programmes can provide employment and improve public facilities. The problem is not lack of money or lack of people with ideas, it is that of how to bring the two together. For too long money has been seen as a force, and not an aid.

Nation-states are units that are often too big to be flexible. I envisage city regions as being the units of taxation, since they would be more responsive to local needs. If city regions were carefully demarcated to minimize disparities in wealth we could have city institutions drawing on local savings and investing in local enterprises. We should be mobilizing local authority pension funds and community group savings so that local capital can help local communities. Investment, enterprise and community need not be separate.

Using Money

The language of money is an important way of 'seeing' places. Cost–benefit analysis, involving the assigning of monetary values to all the likely costs and benefits of a project, is a standard technique. But what constitutes costs and benefits is a difficult decision, and not all costs and benefits can be given an appropriate monetary value. The technique is only as good or as bad as the initial assumptions. Moreover, the people who pay may not be those who benefit. A new airport, for example, may benefit international travellers but not local residents.

When money is used to measure the amount of resources devoted to a particular place, it is a useful device for distributing scarce resources between competing claims and conflicting demands. As a pair of spectacles it yields an impoverished view of the world. When money becomes an end not a means, places suffer from either too little money or too much. 'Cheapskate' places have always existed but in recent years they are particularly evident in government projects such as public housing and some civic buildings. The failure of these places is more the product of a restricted imagination than a tight budget. The problem is not so much the amount of money spent as the way it is allocated. In many public schemes money is spent in ways which benefit the constructors, suit the planners and reflect prestige on the politicians. Many public-housing projects of the 1960s and 1970s were phallic symbols of civic virility rather than sensitive responses to severe housing needs. On that basis some conservatives now argue that all public projects are of doubtful worth. They now want to reduce the welfare role of the state. My response is to argue for a democratization of public projects. This is a mouthful of a slogan, difficult to say and even more difficult to put into practice. What we need are not general public participation exercises, which give a platform to the already articulate, but schemes that give citizens a greater say in the plan preparation, budget formulation and plan implementation in their cities. This involves extra expense, but the costs of getting it wrong are even higher.

As slumps have followed booms in the world economy, the squeeze on the public purse is getting tighter. There are always competing claims and the taxpaying public is always eager to limit expenditure. However, we need to examine the wider social costs and benefits to society of making cities more sensitive to community requirements. The limited funds in the public sphere arise from a mean-minded accountant's view of the world, which sees only the costs of places and not their value. There are enough cost–benefit analyses that can show the costs of doing things. We need a calculus that measures the cost of *not* making places congenial for people. We need to incorporate the wider social costs of vandalism, loneliness, emotional deprivation and social unrest. Of course, we have to be wary of a crude environmental determinism, which simply reads off behaviour directly

Plate 2.6   'Cheapskate' public housing in Glasgow, Scotland: built in the 1960s, abandoned in the 1970s, still being paid for in the 1980s.

from the environment. Social problems and their solutions are only partly related to factors of place. But place is important. If we make urban jungles we should not be surprised that people act like animals.

Some places suffer from too much money. These are the prestige projects. They generally involve numerous committees and the employment of a 'great architect'. Something small and intimate would be seen as demeaning, not a suitable reflection of the importance of the initiating organization. No expense is spared, and the finished project is all glittering glass and burnished concrete with hardwood interiors and marble mosaics in a 'Hey-ma-look-at-me-I-am-an-architect' type of building. Our cities are littered with the detritus of this kind of glory. Such places are more the vehicles for individual, civic, governmental or corporate egos rather than exercises in building workable, liveable places.

Plate 2.7   Prestige blocks in Los Angeles, USA. The metal sculpture is a sure sign that we are in the presence of big-name architects. Even the small amount of public space has to glorify art.

Since the pursuit of grandeur in contemporary urban architecture is measured with reference to existing buildings there is an inbuilt mechanism for increasing size, and a distancing of places from the human scale. The result of this pursuit of unattainable supremacy is a built environment that registers ego rather than soul and reflects private economic power rather than shared social values.

I am not asking for only small buildings to be built. We have a need for grandeur in our lives and buildings have a role to play. What I am suggesting is that we should have greater consultation in how our cities are planned, so that real grandeur can be achieved by the places we collectively decide are so deserving. Big companies should scale down the budget for housing themselves. Let them have their reflected glory, but in the construction of

Plate 2.8   Covent Garden is one of the few human-scale places in
central London. Saved from the worst excesses of office development,
it is a place where people can walk without the fear of traffic or the
intimidation of towering, anonymous office blocks.

places that people will enjoy working in and using. We have to
influence the decision-makers. Let us tell them that their corporate credibility will benefit more from the production of places
sensitive to user preferences. Let us educate them on how to
spend their money. So far, the only people doing this are self-
interested design professionals.

We can take heart from the few successful schemes. A good
case is Covent Garden in central London. The relocation of the
old fruit and vegetable market in the 1960s released a major
site for redevelopment. Like a Monty Python spam lunch, the
first schemes announced in 1968 were the usual dreary mixture
of offices, shops, offices, offices, offices and offices. However, a
group of residents, radical planners and architects formed a

Plate 2.9   Covent Garden, London: the struggle continues.

pressure group, which was ultimately successful in creating a redevelopment where the emphasis was as much on people as profit. The final plan was 'one of sensitive renewal, emphasising rehabilitation and maximising housing, maintenance of the existing community, mixed uses and small scale ... It can only be viewed as a triumph for the defenders of the community, a major reversal for property speculators and developers, and a major concession by the planners' (Christensen, 1981, 121). Today, Covent Garden is one of the delights of Central London, a place of specialized shops, passing crowds and street theatre, where an air of urbanity and charm exists in a place which might have held nothing more than the sterile office blocks. Such successes are few in number and constantly under threat. In 1987 a new plan for Covent Garden was intent on developing more office space. Despite the uphill task, organized groups can save parts of our cities. The forces of capital are many and strong but this side of a complete transformation of society, there is still some purchase to be had from the existing planning if we have the energy, the commitment and the vision. They are *our* cities.

3 Cities as if Only Professionals Matter

... when men think in terms of abstract space rather than real place, of single rather than multiple meanings, and of political aspirations instead of human needs, they tend to produce miles of Jerry-built nowhere.

Robert Hughes
The Shock of the New

The modern welder is now more likely to be a machine than a man. The rise of robotics has dispensed with the skills of whole groups of workers, and even in the office sector the conversation at the end of your telephone is as likely to be a recorded message as a live voice. There has been a deskilling of much skilled and semi-skilled labour. The need for capital to reduce labour costs and the desire to control the labour process has resulted in the automation of whole areas of work. There are, however, some occupational groups who have been able to create or maintain a strong position in the workplace. These are the professionals, traditional ones, such as doctors and lawyers, and emerging groups, such as financial consultants and computer analysts. Their power lies in their ability to influence our perception of the world. Their codes and rationalities govern our lives and affect our cities.

A 'profession' is a group that claims expertise and that can enforce its status through regulation of individual members. Most professions have the traits of assertion and integration. Assertion springs from the need to claim legitimacy. The establishment of the position of expert involves the notion of superior judgement. Doctors, for example, have been very successful in persuading others that they are experts on other people's health. Professional groups claim to have more and better knowledge.

Plate 3.1   Miles of jerry-built nowhere! Brasilia, capital of Brazil, was designed for the motor car rather than for people. The city's structure pays little attention to the realities of Brazilian life, where few people own cars. (Photo courtesy of Peter Hall.)

The integrative element springs from a need to tie their actions and existence to wider social concerns. Few professions say that they are in it for the money. Thus, lawyers argue that theirs is not simply a highly paid profession, but they are the pillars of a system that ensures justice and fairness; similarly, doctors portray themselves as barriers to ill-health and death. According to lawyers and doctors, therefore, only the highly paid legal and medical professions prevent us from returning to the barbarism of the stone age.

Every professional group seems to go through a life-cycle in its relationship with the wider public. Stage one involves the establishment of the profession. Stage two is a 'trust-the-expert' phase, with the corporate body maintaining its reputation. Stage three is the backlash, the 'blame-the-expert' phase, as professional actions fail to meet earlier promises and new circumstances. Bernard Shaw's remark that professions are conspiracies against their customers is appropriate at this stage because it is when professional bodies become even more defensive and try to squash the opposition. The medical profession, for example, in recent years has come under severe criticism from consumers and the alternative medicine movement; their response has been to reiterate their expertise, with reference to its 'scientific' basis and to question the value of alternative health cares.

It would be a major undertaking to look at all professions. Let us look then at the development and status of just two professional groups who have particular importance in the city, architects and planners. Each has a specific story but they are part of that broader history, the emergence of the expert.

The Architects

In the past, there was a dominant image of God as architect. Today it has almost been replaced by the myth of architect as God. It is impossible to identify the architects of Chartres or of Wells cathedral. These were collective endeavours over long periods of time, with a variety of builders and masons working to a common purpose and a shared objective. There was no such thing as 'the architect'. The profession only began to develop with the division of building labour and it was only in the nineteenth and twentieth centuries that architects made a sustained attempt at making themselves a profession. The Institute of British Architects was established in 1834 and received its royal charter in 1837.

On the integrative side, architects began to see themselves as creators of a better way of life. For the romantics, such as John Ruskin, the architect had the job of moral uplift and social purpose. For some of the socialists, architecture was a vehicle for radical social change. Twentieth-century modernist architects, such as Walter Gropius, saw themselves as designers, not just of buildings but of a utopian society.

On the assertive side, architects began to see themselves as

Plate 3.2   Le Corbusier (1887–1965). The architect's original name was Charles Édouard Jeanneret. Any profession whose guru's pseudonym dispenses with the familiarity of a forename while arrogating a definite article must be treated with caution.
© DACS 1988.

arbiters between mere building and 'architecture'. Le Corbusier (1927), one of the most influential of modern architects, decreed that 'Architecture is the masterly correct and magnificent play of masses brought together in light'. Notice that architecture is now art, and the architect by implication an artist, free from the brute demands of an untutored populace. This century has seen the attempted enthronement of the architect as artist, visionary and guru.

Architects grew in status with the growing separation between the users of buildings and the people who commissioned them. Renaissance princes generally lived in the buildings they commissioned, often supervising much of the building work. The modern, bureaucratic, princes, in contrast, have opted for building committees, with architects often given a prominent place. In the private sector, especially since the Second World War, there has been the growth of speculative office blocks, built with no specific client in mind. They were built according to general design considerations, with the voice of the architect becoming more important than the eventual users of the buildings. Discussions have tended to consider aesthetic and budget considerations, rather than the preferences of the users.

As the emphasis has shifted away from client preferences to architectural fashion, the architectural profession has become increasingly arrogant, a posture best summed up in the lecture by Philip Johnson, 'The Seven Crutches of Modern Architecture', given to architectural students at Harvard in 1954 which references Ruskin's *The Seven Lamps of Architecture* (1849). Johnson attacked seven needless crutches of architecture: history, pretty drawing, utility, comfort, cheapness, structure and serving the client. 'It's got to be clear', he told the young students, and a generation of important architects, 'that serving the client is one thing and the art of architecture is another.'

Taking Johnson's advice to heart, modern architecture became strong on commissions, individual reputations and international competitions amongst the cosy few. It was weak on needs, appropriate human scales, social credibility and compassion. A dramatic indication of its social failings was the demolition, in 1972, of the high-rise housing towers of the Pruitt-Igoe scheme in St Louis. The complex had become uninhabitable and no one wanted to live there. The scheme had won an architectural award in 1951. In British cities similar types of high-rise housing are being demolished in the 1980s as local authorities are blowing up buildings less than twenty years old because they are unpopular and uninhabitable.

Le Corbusier, who influenced much of this housing, once said that a building was a machine for living in. The comedian Alexei

Plate 3.3   Pruitt-Igoe, St Louis, Missouri, USA, being demolished. The date, 15 July 1972, perhaps marks the death of optimism in modernist architecture. © *St Louis Post-Dispatch*.

Sayle describes what this really meant to the people of Liverpool: 'They were housed in blocks of flats which resembled giant food processors, electric toothbrushes and hair curling tongs. Baffled and dispirited by living two hundred foot up in the air on an offset lathe or a baked bean canner' (1984, 21–2). It may seem harsh to blame architecture for what are problems of wider social significance, but architects must shoulder some of the responsibility for the production of an alienating urban environment and ultimately an alienated urban population. To be sure, Le Corbusier's vision of residential blocks with communal facilities has been translated into tower blocks without the facilities. His model was done on the cheap and some of the blame must lie with others, but he and other architects had the arrogance to assume that they knew best, that they could design cities and dwellings without reference to citizens and inhabitants.

On Wednesday, 30 May 1984, Prince Charles was asked to speak at a gala dinner of the Royal Institute of British Architects (RIBA). Royalty in Britain are often called upon to say a few words at such occasions: 'Delighted to be here. What a wonderful institution. Keep up the good work.' The usual kind of thing is expected and usually given, but on this particular night Prince Charles did not say the usual kind of thing. He lambasted modern architects for their lack of interest in ordinary people and their concern to design buildings to please other architects rather than the tenants. He criticized the assembled heavies of British architecture for what they had done to the skyline of London. He depicted the extension to the National Gallery in Trafalgar Square as a 'monstrous carbuncle on the face of a much-loved and elegant friend' and described a building in the Mansion House Square as 'another glass giant stump'. He struck a resonant chord with most of his future subjects. Modern architecture is considered by most non-architects as something of a joke. Most buildings given architectural awards are popularly considered to be monstrous failures: too hot in summer, too cold in winter, sometimes leaking and always inconvenient. It is a common belief that buildings which win architectural awards begin to fall apart after two years and send their occupants crazy after four.

Sadly, the response of many architects is to go further into their shells. Seeing themselves as artists and visionaries, they treat

Plate 3.4 Post-Modernism in Architecture *Above*: The Beckman Auditorium, California Institute of Technology, Pasadena, California, USA. Architect: Edward D. Stone. *Below*: Apartment block, Adelaide, Australia. Architect: unknown.

Plate 3.5   Post-Modernism in Architecture   *Above*: St Joseph's
Fountain in Piazza d'Italia, New Orleans, USA. Wham Innovations
Group; architect: Charles Moore. *Below*: Private house in Florence.
Architect: Marco Dezzi Bardesch.

criticism as merely an outburst of philistinism from the ill-informed mob. They like to compare themselves to nineteenth-century artists found wanting by their contemporaries but lauded by later generations. If you have the arrogance to believe that history is on your side then present criticism can safely be ignored.

Popular contempt for architects also springs from their hypocrisy. Walter Gropius, a leading light in the German Bauhaus movement, later a professor of architecture at Harvard and one of the founding fathers of modern architecture, made his reputation in industrial design designing high-density worker housing consisting of large blocks. This was good enough for the workers, but when it came to his own house, Gropius built a low-slung building nestling on a thirty-acre site in the New England countryside. There is the more recent case of Michael Manser, one-time president of RIBA, defender and designer of flat-roofed, high-rise residential blocks. In an interview with a journalist who asked him about these buildings Manser claimed that it was a myth that people didn't like living in them. The interviewer went on: 'I asked him why, if he was such a defender of modern high rise, he himself lived in a nice traditional Georgian house in London. He said, his wife was a passionate gardener, otherwise he might' (Davie, 1983). Such hypocrisy is possible because of the closed nature of architecture. Like most professions it is a modern priesthood; entry is given only after initiation rites, and critics are damned for their audacity or patronized with mild contempt. Architecture separated from its consumers has taken on a life of its own. Modernists' claims and counter-claims and the various voices of post-modernism have developed and declined within a hermetically sealed debating chamber. The design of places has reflected changing professional considerations more than the varied needs of consumers.

The most recent development in architecture is post-modernism. Modernism was the international style of flat-roofed glass boxes, high-rise towers elegant in simplicity, boring in repetition, often lacking any sensitivity to site, location or older buildings. For the architects they were the symbol of a new aesthetic, true to society's needs and honest in relation to materials. For the consumers they came to represent the fashionism of architecture, devoid of any real community involvement in design or layout. Post-modernism uses conscious historical referencing, like the Chippendale high-boy of the AT & T building in New York by Philip Johnson. Post-modernism can be identified by the strong primary colours, arches, tubular decorations, pediments, and the downright whimsy of rococo façades covering factories and baroque entrances to post offices. It is an improvement on the austere asceticism of modernism and some fine buildings have been produced, but it is still a game just for architects, where they can play at spotting the references and identifying the influences; at best, it is a return to a vernacular tradition, at worst, a camp wallow in bad taste, kitsch replacing culture.

The simple conclusion is that the design of buildings and cities is too important to be left only to the architects. Their mistakes endure long after they have passed on to the next lucrative contract, the next architects' conference or the next showing of their designs to a small, select band of fellow architects. Our cities have become the graveyards of outdated architectural theories. The giant glass towers, once the buildings of the future, are now the tombstones of architectural modernism.

The Planners

Urban planning has a long history. Cities have been planned from the Egyptians to the Aztecs and from Imperial Rome to Renaissance Europe. Urban planning as a profession has its roots in the massive urbanization of the nineteenth century when villages became towns, towns became cities and cities became major urban regions. In 1800 there were no cities in Europe with a population greater than a million; but by 1900 there were nine, four of them in Britain: London, Manchester, Birmingham and Glasgow. The demand for planning came from several sources. There were the civic authorities, who wanted cleaner, safer, more efficient cities. There were the business groups, who wanted to off-load on to the state some of the costs of production and reproduction, such as housing for the workers and transport for people and goods. And there were the reformers, who condemned the urban squalor. For them, the city was the cause of social unrest and planning was more than just a technical exercise; it was a vehicle for improving life chances and ensuring

Plate 3.6 Early town planning: Louis XIV commanding the planning of the Hôtel des Invalides, Paris.
(Source: Dayot, Armand (1909), *Louis XIV, Illustrations d'après des Peintures, sculptures, gravures, objets, etc., du temps*, Flammarion, Paris.)

social stability. The drive for efficiency, material interest, fear of social conflict and the desire for social reform have all shaped the early development of planning and have continued to exercise an influence.

The adoption of various urban planning measures in North America and Western Europe was strengthened by several factors: There was growing recognition that the state could and should become involved in the urban arena. The development of planning reflected and marked the acceptance of the need to regulate property rights. In addition, various urban planning experiments set an example. Robert Owen's at New Lanark in Scotland at the end of the eighteenth century was one of the best-known examples of a planned community for factory workers attracting visitors from all over Europe. Similar schemes were established in North America, with Alexander Hamilton and the Society for Establishing Useful Manufactures founding the model town of Paterson in New Jersey. Later schemes, such as Port Sunlight on Merseyside, Bourneville outside Birmingham and Pullman, near Chicago, confirmed the economic benefits of a well-housed labour force; they showed what planned towns could do for social harmony and return on investment.

The reforming impulse was helped by the development of a discourse about urban planning. The planning reformers successfully lobbied governments and the ensuing legislative measures created a demand for planners. The British Town Planning Institute was established in 1914, five years after the 1909 Housing and Town Planning Act, which gave planning powers to local authorities; the American City Planning Institute was formed in 1917 after several cities had developed zoning ordinances regulating land use.

Early urban planning theorists had radical roots and utopian visions as well as pragmatic policies. To achieve their goals they used the state. In return, planning has always been closely linked to the requirements of the state. The growth of the profession was enmeshed in the bureaucratic system of government practice, and the general tendency has been for plans combining social reform and civic design to be shorn of their radicalism and, if implemented, restricted to physical design. Governments have, in most cases, evaporated the radical ideas of social change leaving behind the residue of civic design.

The case of Ebenezer Howard will serve as an illustration. In 1898 he published *Garden Cities of Tomorrow*, reissued four years later as *Tomorrow: A Peaceful Path to Real Reform*. He suggested that the advantages of urban and rural environments could be combined in garden cities, new towns where the fresh air of the countryside could be combined with the job opportunities of the city. The land was to be held by the community so that any increase in value, and hence rents, could be used for the provision of municipal services. Howard sought to turn his ideas into reality. In 1902 he founded the Garden City Pioneer Company which bought 4,000 acres in Hertfordshire. The first new town was Letchworth. In 1920 the second town of Welwyn Garden City was founded. Howard's ideas were taken up by various people, such as F. J. Osborn and Lewis Mumford, and given institutional form in the Town and Country Planning Association (TCPA). For those who see no role for idealistic pressure groups the TCPA is a salutary reminder of their success. During the inter-war period they lobbied for new towns in Britain and in 1946 the New Towns Act established fourteen new towns between 1946 and 1950. Another eighteen were set up after 1950. The success, however, was limited to design matters. The community control of land as envisaged by Howard was watered down. New towns in the UK are examples of civic design that did not become social experiments. Government involvement housed 2 million people in the UK in New Towns but it did not lead to an alternative system of landownership. State power can turn dreams into reality, but often at a cost to the radicalism of the original visions.

Until the 1960s urban planning was dominated in theory and practice by the concept of end-point master plans, in which preferred land-use configurations informed policy decisions. The planner's role involved designing a physical plan for the city and coordinating the decisions of the various public bodies (such as electricity, gas and water services, education and social services) so that the plan could be achieved. Since the 1960s, the concept of the master plan has come under criticism. Rosy assumptions about economic growth, population projections, family size and fuel costs proved to be wildly inaccurate and there was mounting criticism about top-down, non-participatory forms of planning. With their master plans taken away from them, the planners

Plate 3.7 Ebenezer Howard (1850–1928), founder of the Garden City
Movement. © Town and Country Planning Association.

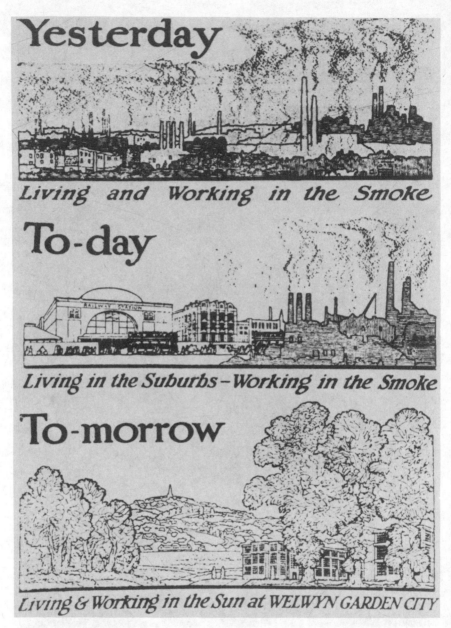

Plate 3.8 Publicity poster to attract people to Welwyn Garden City, outside London.

(Source: Tod, I. and Wheeler, M. (1978), *Utopia*, Orbis, London.)

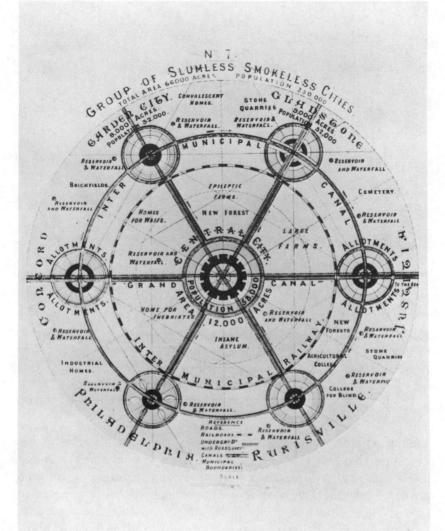

Plate 3.9 Urban vision 1: Model garden cities by Ebenezer Howard.
(Source: Howard (1898), *Tomorrow: A Peaceful Path to Real Reform*, Swan
Sonnenschein, London.)

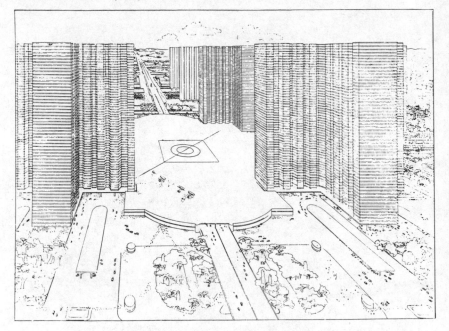

Plate 3.10   Urban vision 2: 'Plan for the 3 million city' – The city of
tomorrow as envisaged by Le Corbusier in 1924.
(Source: Le Corbusier (1924) *Urbanisme*, Editions Crés, Paris. Translated into
English as *The City of To-morrow* in 1929.) © DACS 1988.

sought, chameleon-like, to maintain a role for themselves by
changing their ideas to suit the changing circumstances. In the
1960s planners were concerned with redistributing economic
growth; by the 1980s they were concerned with generating
growth.

Some theorists began to question the role and purpose of planning. The 1970s saw powerful critiques arguing that planning
benefited those who were already powerful, and that urban planning was not an innocent activity devoid of social meaning and
redistributional consequences. This line of attack, while it did a
valuable job of demystifying planning, could do little more than
criticize the status quo. Now we have a practice firmly rooted in
routine government action and radical theories weak on prescription. Planners, who guide the infrastructure necessary to attract

employment, do not ask about the quality of jobs, and the radical theorists do little more than criticize the establishment bias of current planning practice. Both groups lack a vision of planning and have failed to inform the debate about what makes good and fair cities where people can lead creative and dignified lives.

Use the Expert

We cannot put all the blame on the experts. Professional groups have taken over responsibility and gained power because we have neglected responsibility and given them power. We have given up control of too much of our public and private lives, partly because of constraints – we all have other pressing demands on our time – but partly by choice. There is a strong belief that someone else will fix things, and we have too much deference for professional groups. The development of the expert is a function of the creation of the non-expert.

We need a democratization of expertise, a recognition that technical skills are important but they do not entitle people to order our reality. We need to unmask the jargon of professionals and decipher their languages of obfuscation. Education has an invaluable role to play in building up people's individual self-confidence and encouraging their collective social power. Let us have fewer stories of great men and more about how we all have the ability to create our own individual and collective realities. Perhaps we will then be able to identify a fourth stage in the cycle of professions. After the stages of establishment of the expert, trusting the expert and blaming the expert, perhaps we might see the emergence of the stage of using the experts, without deferring to them.

In their relationship with the wider public both architects and planners are still at the third stage. Criticisms of architects and planners are now the very stuff of journalism, but we cannot pin all the blame for our present cities just on these professions. We have to move beyond a simple condemnation to the fourth stage of using the experts. Solutions lie not in dispensing with experts but in a proper utilization of their skills.

In the case of architects we have to bring them back into

popular discourse. Lacking a firm basis in popular participation, too much architecture is bereft of social purpose; more about individual egos than collective goals, it is strong on what makes architects different from the rest of us, weak on how architects can make things better. Architects and architecture need to become part of a wider public discussion. We need a socialization of the debate about the form and nature of our buildings. We need to encourage architects to be concerned with the social quality of their buildings. Architects should inform, but not dominate, debates about present and future cities. There is a need for greater public participation in architecture.

The planners have been less successful than the architects in claiming a privileged position. Their success, and our problem, is their almost total integration with established power and government practice. Planning practice has become too establishment while planning theory has become too marginal. The practitioners are now firmly rooted in the mundane world of everyday responses, while the theorists are in the stratosphere of intellectual fashion. The result is a practice without vision, and a theory without popular support. But planners do have a role between these two extremes. There is a genuine need for informed discussion on matters of physical design, civic layout and appropriate environmental contexts for different social events. The era of the master plan emanating from the single visionary is over, and rightly so. Those master plans represented an imposition on people who had little say in their design or implementation. Planning informed by popular discussion does have a continuing relevance. Planners need to reinsert themselves into popular debates about good cities and better societies.

To create better cities we need architects who can design interesting, liveable spaces and planners who can provide life-enhancing plans. Not all professionals work against the creation of more humane cities. The election of Rod Hackney to the Presidency of RIBA marks an institutional victory for the concept of community architecture, and there are a host of planners helping with the sorts of community plan that I mentioned in the last chapter, for example Covent Garden. We cannot dismiss all architects and planners just as we cannot dispense with their skills. We need to encourage those professionals who use their skills in the pursuit of broader, shared social objectives.

Plate 3.11   Architects and planners don't always get it wrong. The Sydney Opera House, Australia, completed in 1972 and designed by the Dane Joern Utzon, is one of those buildings that have the constant ability to elicit wonder.

If we ask too much of our architects and too little of our planners we can only be disappointed. They do have a role; they can inform public debate, provide expertise and raise matters of aesthetic alternatives and technical feasibility. An informed citizenry in association with imaginative professionals provides us with perhaps the best basis for constructing pleasing buildings and liveable cities. Like all professional groups they seek public recognition. We can give them this without denying them professional credibility or abrogating our collective responsibility. Our cities are too important to be left to the 'experts'.

4 Cities as if Only Some People Matter

> ... the city exists for one particular kind of citizen: the adult, male, white-collar, out of town car-user.
>
> Colin Ward
> *The Child in the City*

Cities give physical expression to relations of power in society. The population of cities is very varied; citizens can be rich, poor, young, old, men and women, but these diverse experiences, needs and aspirations are not given equal weight in our cities. In this chapter I will examine those groups marginalized by their poverty, their stage in the life-cycle and their gender.

Rich Cities and Poor Citizens

There are some cities that are better than others to live in if you are rich, but there is a disheartening similarity about the experience of the poor in all cities. Poverty is not simply low income, it is an inability to influence outcomes in a regular and meaningful way. The poor are the alienated of the city both in their feeling of powerlessness and their sense of estrangement from the wider society. When poverty is more the product of personal characteristics, the result is the individual poor, the park-bench occupants, the winos on the corner, the inhabitants of the doss-houses, the citizens of Cardboard City. These are individual tragedies to be ameliorated by care and counselling. Our concern should be to lessen their suffering and provide opportunities for the creation and maintenance of self-respect. When alienation affects whole groups of citizens, the result is an underclass, a 'lumpenproletariat', as Marx described the unskilled workers of urban Victorian

Britain. The unemployed blacks of the ghetto are a more recent example. The distinction between atomized and structured group poverty is not precise. The atomized poor tend to come more from the disadvantaged than the advantaged groups in society. There are fewer brain surgeons sleeping on park benches (on a regular basis) than unskilled labourers. We have to be wary of ignoring structural factors, but we must also be careful of making them the only explanation. Not all blacks are unemployed.

There are three popular responses to the urban poor. The first is to *blame the poor*. The fault, so the argument goes, lies with the poor themselves: their characteristics, their behaviour or their attitudes. There is a grain of truth in the argument. An alienated group can become disheartened and discouraged. This is a response to alienation, not its cause. The blame-the-poor ideology ignores the wider context and takes consequences for causes. The poor act the way they do because they are poor; they are not poor because of the way they act.

The second response is to *romanticize the poor*: to see them as heroic victims. Such a view, common amongst those who feel guilty about their affluence, tends to disregard the stultifying effect of poverty and its distortion on individual development. There is no romance to poverty, it is destructive of self-respect and a blight on our society.

The third, and most common, response is to *ignore the poor*. This is the easiest strategy for the rich to adopt; it involves little more than a closing of the eyes or an adjustment of the view to encompass a more pleasing prospect.

The poor fail to register their voice in the public policy arena: they are poor for this very reason. The atomized poor constitute a nuisance more than a social threat. They provide the basis for embarrassing interactions: when some battered face asks me for money, either I give it quickly, in a hurry to get the transaction over as fast as possible, or I hurry past with eyes downcast. Both actions make me feel equally guilty. The structured poor, in contrast, constitute a social force and have on occasions taken to the streets. Urban rioting has many causes and innumerable roots. After the riots in the inner cities of Britain in 1981 the government set up a public inquiry under Lord Scarman. The Scarman Report (1981) noted that many young people in the inner city were denied opportunities and the riots could be seen as a 'burst of anger'. To ignore the poor for too long is to run the risk of such anger.

It is difficult to identify easy solutions. It is easier to see two common mistakes. The first is to see the solution in more policing, a common response of politicians reacting to public disquiet at televised disorder. However, the cry for more policing does not deal with causes; its main function is reaffirmation of political leadership and social control. The second mistake is to see riots simply as the response to broad economic and political forces: unemployment equals riots, and less public expenditure means more alienation. This approach fails to explain why some unemployed people riot and others don't.

Some would argue that nothing less than the complete overthrow of the present system will solve the problems of the urban poor; the real problem, however, lies in power relations. If there is a route between waiting for the great day or telling people to accept their lot, then one possible direction is to encourage people to achieve more power over their own lives and neighbourhoods. We can begin by listening to people – not only to what they want, but what they can do, what they can contribute. If we see the urban underclass not as the problem but the solution then we can begin to concentrate on creating the preconditions for self-respect and dignity. Local communities working with skilled professionals can make a move in the right direction by harnessing local resources and local talents. The problems will be many, from everyday difficulties to the global power relations over which local communities will have little control or influence. The flows of international capital, for example, are unlikely to be affected by the demands for jobs in a local area. But rather than throw up our hands and bemoan the fact, we have to use the skills of local people to propose feasible alternatives to unemployment, perhaps involving the encouragement of informal economies and neighbourhood networks. Ultimately, it should involve a decentralization of control. The top-down relation found in the British reliance on professional community workers getting poor people to know their rights may be a useful start but eventually it needs to be replaced by organizations which get people to exercise their own rights. The work of Saul Alinsky (1969, 1972) shows how poor neighbourhoods can get things done when they organize around specific attainable goals. The

Alinsky emphasis on self-interest is a powerful mobilizer of local opinion and interest. It ignores wider causes and hidden needs, but as a kick-start to local action it is second to none.

Whatever the question, Lenin is reputed to have said, the answer is always power. In their collective presence the poor have power and can exercise it; after all, they have less to lose and more to gain than everyone else. If this power is channelled by good organization and sound information (intellectuals have a role to play here) then poor people can gain some control over their own neighbourhoods. It is only with such control that they can begin to effect liveable, appropriate responses to global forces.

Trouble in Autopia

One of the most obvious changes in urban structure over the last two hundred years has been the spread of the city. There has been a change from a *pedestrian city*, limited in size by walking distances, through the era of the *mass transit city* to the contemporary *auto city*. The car is now the major means of passenger transport. In 1900 there was only one car registered for every 10,000 people in the USA; by 1980 it was one car for every two people. Cities have been massively transformed by the automobile, with urban sprawl, motorways and traffic hold-ups, only the most obvious effects. In the USA almost 60,000 people die every year in motor accidents. In the UK the figure is 5,000. The daily slaughter on our roads is a disgrace made all the worse by the seeming acceptance of the carnage as an acceptable price to be paid for the advantages of the motor car.

The introduction of the motor car has brought tremendous benefits, but the cost of increased personal mobility has been cities designed more for cars than for people. Car-users have had their needs placed at the top of the transport-planning agenda, public-transport solutions have been relegated to second-best solutions and pedestrians and bike riders have to fight to get safe passage through the city. As J. M. Thomson (1977, 15) notes:

> Most of the people professionally responsible for urban transport are car owners and drive to their offices everyday. The most powerful transport highway authorities are usually highway

Plate 4.1   One of the costs of the motorway solution is increased
pollution. This is a smog station in Los Angeles, USA.

engineering departments occupying premises provided with free
parking space to which most of the senior staff commute by car.
The senior managers of public transport companies are more
likely to arrive by car than one of their own buses. And one of the
first tasks of a team of consultants engaged to undertake an urban
transport study is to acquire a fleet of private cars. It is beyond
dispute that most important decisions affecting urban transport
are made by people whose personal viewpoint of the problem is
largely behind the wheel of a car.

As the city has spread out, different land uses have become more
and more segregated. In the pedestrian city most people could get
to work, buy goods and go to the ale house, on foot. Now most
jobs are in the commercial or industrial zones, shops are in the
retail districts, and people leave their residential areas to be enter-
tained. The car has allowed these land uses to be disentangled

and dispersed throughout the city. But car access is not universal and three groups have been disadvantaged:

households who do not own a car. Even in rich cities this can amount to over 60 per cent of households;

certain members of car-owning households. There is an unequal access to private transport even within car-owning households. Surveys of an inner London suburb showed that while almost one-half of all households had a car, only one-quarter of all adults had independent access to one (Hillman et al., 1976). The typical case is for the wage-earner to use the car to drive to work, leaving those at home without access to a car. Only the richer families can afford two or more cars;

people who are unable to use a motor-vehicle because of age limits, and those with physical or mental disabilities. The young, the old and the infirm have no independent access to private motor transport.

All three groups have been affected by the widespread use of the motor car. Adolescents have difficulty getting to places in the city without drawing on the time of their parents, the non-car-user in a car-owning family may find it difficult to look for jobs outside a very small area around their place of residence and non-car-owning families have limited opportunities for travel. Lack of accessibility has real effects on employment prospects and overall quality of life.

The urban motorways of the 1960s and 1970s only addressed the concerns of the car-user, and even in this respect they were only partial solutions. Their construction generated more traffic, they were expensive, and they involved the destruction of existing communities as neighbourhoods were sacrificed so that the better-off could enjoy improved accessibility.

There are three ways of helping the carless: reducing the cost of cars, improving public transport or reordering the city. The first option creates problems of congestion and pollution; longer-term solutions therefore must involve the second two ways. Imaginative public transport schemes of recent years include:

the Labour Party's 'Fares Fair' policy in London between 1982 and 1984 of reducing fares and improving existing bus and tube services to reverse the downward spiral of low use – high fares – low use. The result was reduction of congestion and greater use of tube trains and buses;

high-tech solutions, as in California where San Francisco developed a mass transit scheme – BART (Bay Area Rapid Transit);

the experiment of some Japanese cities with medium-capacity transport systems involving monorails, light railways and automated guidance transit systems.

Whatever the scheme adopted it seems that few public transport schemes are self-financing. The necessary subsidies can become an easy target for criticism and political point-scoring. It is important, however, to consider all the costs and benefits of alternative transport schemes. The high energy costs of private car usage, the congestion, accidents, air pollution and the need for adequate parking are all hidden costs, which need to be uncovered in any comparison of public and private schemes. However, we also have to be wary of getting involved in the sterile public–private debate. The real question is not the choice between public and private but how we make private transport (which has a lot of benefits) less antisocial and less expensive, and how we ensure that public transport (which has many constraints) becomes more responsive to client preferences and needs.

I do not think that sustainable urban transport solutions lie in producing more cars or developing expensive high-tech transport systems. More realistic solutions are to be found in cheap transport systems informed by everyday users. It is surely not beyond our collective imagination to provide cheap, reliable and regular transport systems without polluting our environment, using up finite resources or killing our fellow citizens?

Demand for transport arises because activities are located in different parts of the city. We also need to reorder the city so that there is less need for costly movement. Much twentieth-century planning is based on the urban experience of the nineteenth century. For example, a central tenet of modern planning is the desired separation of the workplace from the home. This aim was commendable at a time when workplaces were noisy, dirty,

Plate 4.2 Mass transit schemes come in different vintages and styles: trams in Melbourne, Australia (*above*), and BART in San Francisco, California, USA (*below*).

smelly places. It is less relevant now, when modern industry can be less noisy than the average lawnmower. No one would suggest locating a chemical factory in a housing estate, but if we were to treat each case on its merits rather than make blanket controls for the rigid separation of industrial and residential land uses, then our land-use control system might be flexible enough to encourage non-polluting, neighbour-friendly activities in residential areas. A more cellular city with a wider dispersal at the local level of shopping, recreational and employment opportunities would minimize much of the need for transport. We can make a start by insisting on a mix of activity spaces in any new developments.

Stages in the Life-Cycle

The most powerful people in the city are the middle-aged men who operate the institutions that make and transform cities. Their needs and preferences are accepted as the community standard, yet the city contains other people, at different stages in the life-cycle, whose needs and preferences are always secondary and often ignored.

The typical person is very dependent on older people from the time of birth until about the age of two or three; in later childhood, from about two to twelve, there is greater scope and ability for independent movement; adolescence follows, then adulthood, and finally old age. The categories are rough indicators, not precise demarcations: I have met some adults who have never grown up and some children who were aged eight going on fifty-four. The extent to which these categories are more socially defined than biologically determined is an important topic, but one whose exposition is beyond the scope of this chapter.

Early Childhood

Our cities are not very responsive to the needs of children or people with children. Transport systems, to take just one example, tend to be designed for single users. Ample demonstration is available to anyone who has seen a young mother with two shopping bags and a child in a pushchair trying to get on or off a bus. Encouraging the decentralization of services, retail establishments and employment opportunities could reduce the transport difficulties for adults with children.

We could also do more to shift the awesome burden of constant childrearing from the shoulders of individuals, usually women, by providing crèches and kindergartens. Extending childcare facilities does not necessarily imply more public spending. One possibility is to foster self-help childcare schemes. Lack of money is sometimes a problem in getting these schemes established but, more commonly, problems result from a combination of lack of money and lack of organizational ability. Informal networks are prone to collapse if leading figures leave; local authorities can help by providing continuity in the basic organizational jobs of contacting people and getting roster duties arranged. Many other suggestions would be forthcoming if the concerned groups were consulted. Proper care and attention of children does not necessarily involve a great deal of public spending, but it does involve listening to those who have responsibility for infants. At the moment parents and parent-figures are not consulted often enough. The city has been planned primarily as a source of employment, with scant regard for it as a place for human nurture and personal growth.

Late Childhood

Late childhood sees the development of motor skills, and the ability to move beyond the front door without adult assistance. Children have a capacity and a need for exploration; it is a source of play and a way of increasing knowledge of themselves and their surroundings. We have a responsibility to make safe and interesting environments for people at this stage of development, yet children are locked out of much of urban life. Our cities fail our children, particularly the children of less advantaged parents. Pollution, for example, affects all citizens, but it affects children most of all: they breathe in more air per unit of body weight than do adults, they are more physically active, they are more likely to breathe through their mouths and they are closer to the ground where the pollutants lie. Only in a society where children are marginalized could the exhaust pipes of most cars be in perfect alignment with the average height of a toddler.

Children need to explore the confines of the home. We need to make sure, therefore, that the immediate environment around the home is safe. A clearer separation between pedestrians and motor traffic is one important prerequisite. Every year in Britain about 800 children are killed and 40,000 are injured. The figures could be reduced if more residential areas were freed from the tyranny of through traffic. We also need a change in attitude: 'If a child hits a car, it's vandalism; but if a car hits a child, it's an accident' (Michelson et al., 1979, vol. 2, 234). We need to move from accident designation towards greater driver responsibility, so that people, not traffic, become the main factor in city design.

Children need to be protected from people as well as from machines; we need to create defensible spaces, open areas that the local community can watch, so that self-policing becomes a deterrent to crime and vandalism. Such spaces allow younger children to play in relative safety. Oscar Newman (1973) has shown how even small design improvements, such as the construction of fences and the use of boundary markers, can be important. We should allow children to make their own defensible spaces.

Adolescence

Adolescence is an awkward transition between the very different worlds of child and adult, and there are few formal opportunities in the city for adolescents to express their existence. There are too few planned spaces for people of this age: playgrounds are beneath them, nightclubs and bars are (legally) beyond them. City authorities rarely use the tremendous energy that this group of people possesses, and in general we provide too few opportunities for young people to get involved in the life of the city. We are only fair to our children when we do not treat them as children. I once saw a city farm in an inner area of Bristol where children were involved in looking after animals on a formerly derelict site. It was probably the least vandalized place I have ever seen. The reason was because it was the children's own place: they had some control, some responsibility and a sense of engagement. Good cities encourage and foster these feelings.

Plate 4.3 Adolescents are given few formal opportunities in the city. They have to make their own spaces in public parks, shopping malls and the like. This group of young people is sitting around in a public park in Bristol, UK.

The Final Years

In advanced capitalist countries the population is ageing. Even in a 'young' country, like Australia, the median age has increased from twenty-two in 1901 to a projected thirty-four in the year 2000. As life expectancy increases and the birth-rate declines, the proportion of the population aged over sixty-five rises. By the end of this century the over-sixty-fives will comprise almost one-quarter of the total population in richer countries. This demographic shift has major implications. A declining workforce, for example, will have to support an increasing number of retirees. Moreover, ageism is as virulent a process of social stigmatization as sexism or racism. The predominant response is to encourage the disengagement of the elderly from the rest of the community. Yet by locking up our older generation in old folks' homes, we deny them dignity and a functioning role in society. As Lewis Mumford (1968, 41) notes: 'The aged find their lives progressively curtailed and meaningless, while their days are ironically lengthened.' Elderly people make many contributions. In a survey of 938 elderly households in Sydney, Hal Kendig (1984) found that 45 per cent contributed to other households in the form of childminding, transport provision, meal preparation and gardening. The author concluded, that, contrary to popular opinion,

> most older people are more likely to be providing than receiving support in many areas of life ...
>
> .   .   .   .   .
>
> An accurate portrayal of older people's contributions can counteract the self-fulfilling label of older people as necessarily being dependent, and burdens on their families and government. It can improve self-image and respect, provide role models for would-be contributors, and encourage the needy aged to accept assistance as an earned right justified by earlier contributions. (Kendig, 1984, 96)

We fail to tap fully the enormous resources in the elderly population. By locking them away, we reject years of accumulated knowledge, talent, experience and wisdom. We can make moves in this direction according to Kendig by

> developing programs for older volunteers and launching publicity campaigns to break down entrenched stereotypes. As people retire earlier and live longer, it should be possible to redefine old age as a time of contributing in ways which were limited in mid life. Acknowledging and fostering contributions by older people may well be a necessary part of the process of redistributing power and its attendant privileges and opportunities.

We can do much by encouraging a greater mix in residential areas. Some elderly people need sheltered housing but this can be located beside single-person and larger family-type dwellings in developments in such a way as to allow people a measure of privacy while allowing opportunities for community encounters. Mixed residential areas provide the environmental preconditions for a greater integration of the elderly into community life. By

using the abilities of the elderly, and by encouraging their contributions, we extend the range of our social experience and
improve the quality of our social life.

Women in Men-Made Cities

Cities and buildings are, by and large, designed by men – even in
spheres where women are important. While most domestic
labour is still performed by women, house design still reflects
men's ideas rather than women's experience. Kitchens are often
poorly designed and although there may be work rooms and
family rooms in the typical house, little space is set aside for the
recreational use of women. As the authors of a study of public
housing in Britain concluded: 'In the final decision-making,
women's real needs, desires and aspirations are not taken as
seriously as male-dominated ideas about the "appropriate" house
for the family' (Matrix, 1984, 80). The bulk of housing is for the
individualized consumption of families, each dwelling having its
own kitchen, laundry, bathroom, etc. This form of housing maximizes the amount of domestic labour and, because of the predominant household division of labour, maximizes the work of
each woman, reinforces women's domestic role and strengthens
patriarchal relations. Even access to housing is structured. For
many women adequate shelter is only possible through linking
up with a man, and continued shelter may involve continued
attachment.
   Overcoming the oppression of women requires more than the
rearrangement of our houses, neighbourhoods and cities. Complete emancipation involves a transformation of the existing relations of power. In the meantime, however, there are some, albeit
small, things that can be done in terms of civic design. The most
obvious is that women should be consulted in the design and layout of housing and neighbourhoods. Fundamental questions of
user preference, accessibility and safety will thus be highlighted.
There is a real need to feminize the city; for too long now it has
borne only the imprint of male perceptions and male power. There
is a possible contradiction in this programme: to become involved
in design issues may improve the relative public position of
women but it may also reinforce their role as domestic labourers.

Plate 4.4   This statue in Vienna, Austria, depicts women as passive objects of desire. Many cities embody this image in more than just statues.

The tension is made all the more acute because housework for many women permits greater control over the level, pace and timing of labour than formal employment, and may provide a more rewarding experience than waged labour. This tension can be partially resolved if women are given greater choice. This could involve:

encouraging communal, as opposed to individual, care of the young and the elderly. Experiments with playgroups and grandparent-minding schemes may free women from some of their current burdens;

encouraging housing designs with such features as communal kitchens, and laundries and childminding spaces. Again, such schemes may lighten the loads of domestic labour;

encouraging the role of women in the design professions; with the added provisos mentioned in the previous chapters. We would gain little of we simply replaced male experts with female experts.

There are many people in the city whose voices are rarely heard. They live in a city of other people's making. Ultimately we need to incorporate these other voices, we need to feminize the city, and encourage the engagement of the young and old; we need cities which reflect the needs and preferences of all citizens. If not, we impoverish our cities and our society. The real wealth of a city lies in the collective and individual creativity of all its citizens.

Part II
Ideas for Cities as if People Matter

We are at the end of an epoch, when every old category begins to have a hollow sound, and when we are groping in the dark to discover the new. Some of us must be content to offer unfinished 'Notes'.

E. P. Thompson
Exterminism Reviewed

5 Towards Better Cities

The town presents the single raw material of local proximity out of which municipal life is to be built. The first business of the municipal reformer then is to transform this excessive proximity into wholesome neighbourhood, in order that true neighbourly feelings may have a room to grow and thrive, and eventually to ripen into the flower of a fair civic life ... to evoke the personal human qualities of this medley of city workers so as to reach within the individual the citizen, to educate the civic feeling until it takes shape in civic activities and institutions, which not only safeguard the public welfare against the encroachments of private industrial agreed, but shall find an ever ampler and nobler expression in the aesthetic beauty and spiritual dignity of a complex, common life – all this work of transformation lies in front of the democracy, grouped in its ever-increasing number of town-units.

J. A. Hobson
The Evolution of Modern Capitalism

On Looking into the Future

All thoughts about future states of society and the various urban possibilities should engage the issues of means and ends, and timescales.

It is a mistake to assume that radical ends are always achieved by radical means. Society needs reordering so as to create more humane cities, but through a collective endeavour in which people have the opportunity to change the circumstances of their own lives. The experience of the twentieth century has shown us the dangers and limitations of social change instigated from above. Top-down socialism in backward countries has tended to produce backward socialism. More lasting and beneficial changes to the lives of ordinary people come from enabling them to develop confidence in their individual and collective abilities. The ideal mix is one in which enlightened top-down changes enhance the purchase of bottom-up social progress.

We can identify an unspecified *future*, a closer *soon* and a more immediate *tomorrow*. Visions of the future need to be tied to appropriate timescales – what may be fine for the future, may be impractical to achieve by tomorrow. My ultimate goal is the humane city of the future but the emphasis here is on shorter-term means. I do not present a fully worked-out model of an ideal social order: rather, I seek to identify better means for 'tomorrow' and 'soon'.

We can begin to think about better cities in a number of ways. We could, for example, establish a set of ends (or goals) which most of us could subscribe to: good housing for all, minimum wages, adequate public services, etc. We could also lay down some basic criteria for the design of cities to enhance and achieve these ends: for example a better mix of residential and non-residential land uses. These are important discussions and ones where architects, community groups, planners, economists and others can make important contributions. In this book, however, I am more interested in the quality of the means by which we achieve these ends than in the end product. I am concerned in this second part of the book, therefore, more with means than with ends. This takes me beyond a discourse of environmental design and broad goals and into discussions of the quality of political participation, the nature of welfare provisions and the importance of work. There are other important issues, but we cannot speak about good cities without at least discussing these three themes. The city is both a cause and an effect of such social arrangements.

Technology and Social Relations

The creation of better cities involves changing many things. Technological solutions are often touted. Technology can improve our lives – ask anyone who now uses a washing machine when before they had a scrubbing board and a thick bar of green soap. I hold no illusions about a less-technical world. A world with fewer labour-saving gadgets only means that some people have to do more work. But we must be wary of a technological determinism that believes in the quick, easy technical-fix to our social ills. The optimism shown about the fifth-generation computers is comparable to a belief in the Second Coming. Technology alone cannot solve our problems; it can have regressive as well as progressive implications. Computers may provide us with beneficial things, such as expert systems of medical diagnosis, but they can also be used by the state to monitor the activities of dissident citizens. The myth of the machine as saviour provides the illusion of a conflict-free method of resolving our social difficulties. Social questions, not technical concerns, are at the heart of improvements in our social affairs. In the following chapters I will ignore debates about technology; they are important but not central. The creation of better cities fundamentally involves questions about the shape and quality of social relations.

On Ideas

Ideas reflect the climate of the times. We live in a time of cynicism, and a whole tradition of liberal thinking and emancipatory politics is now under attack. Life-enhancing beliefs are criticized as idealist or marginalized as utopian; greed and selfishness are cloaked in the language of realism and practicality. I repudiate this unidimensional view of human nature. Cynicism is a lack of imagination not a full assessment of human potential; the present conditions tax the liberal imagination, but they do not invalidate it.

The twentieth century has traumatized the imagination. The Bomb, the Holocaust, the incessant imagery of starvation, violence and war threaten to wash away our conception of human goodness and social responsibility. To accept cynicism is understandable; it is an easy option. It must be understood, however, that it is a retreat and not a full survey. There is nothing inherently 'realistic' and 'practical' about jettisoning moral values and beliefs in social progress; the language is used deliberately to disguise the greed and selfishness that lie at the root of social inequalities. In the era of macho monetarism, the people who speak about tough decisions are not those who face the unpleasant consequences.

Empowerment and Engagement

All around us can be seen schools that do not encourage pupils fully to develop their abilities, companies that suppress the creativity of their employees and cities that have no place for the goodwill and knowledge of their citizens. The major argument of this book is that better cities can be created if all citizens are both *empowered* and *engaged*. Empowerment is a simple concept: it implies giving more power to individuals over the compass of their lives through better administrative structures and improved social arrangements. It should be possible to set mutually acceptable limits to individual empowerment that do not impinge on the rights of others.

Engagement implies the involvement of people in all the various activities of their public life and a democratization in the way we arrive at social goals. I believe there is a deep human need for engagement. People require a sense of linkage with others in their community, and society can benefit from enhancing and encouraging these connections because they increase the range of human talents and creativity. Individuals can best realize their creative power and achieve greater self-esteem in a social context.

Engagement can take two forms: *goal-formulation* allows people to be involved in setting social priorities, and *implementation* involves turning these goals into reality. There are different levels of engagement, from manipulative incorporation, through tokenism, to direct reflections of public power. As used here, the term 'engagement' means real participation involving direct public control, delegated responsibility or power-sharing.

Let me highlight the theme of engagement with an example drawn from my own experience. From 1979 to 1981 I taught an undergraduate course on political geography to a third-year group at Reading University. In the first two years students were graded by results obtained in the conventional three-hour exam. The system was unsatisfactory because it did not develop the students' own critical faculties and, for me, exam marking con-

Plate 5.1   The view from the executive suite of the Hilton Hotel in Sydney, Australia, shows buildings and streets; it fails to register people.

sisted of reading what I had said in lectures, transmitted through the hand of the student. The whole point of the exercise seemed to be a power relationship, not an encouragement of their intellectual growth. Subsequently students were asked to write essays on topics of their own choice. The result was an array of essays that ranged from good to excellent. They were interesting to read and, by most accounts, interesting to write. The students had been given some control in implementation and, to a lesser extent, goal-formulation. The outcome was a vast improvement over the old command relationship of formal examinations.

Full engagement involves both goal-formulation and implementation. There are many instances of partial engagement, generally involving implementation rather than formulation. The above example allowed students more freedom to exercise their talents, but in a structured context that was geared towards ranking them, a goal in which they had little say and for which they perhaps had little sympathy. Partial engagement may allow some exercise of creativity and is not to be dismissed out of hand, but full engagement is the desired state.

Empowerment and engagement are related: empowerment without engagement is power without responsibility; engagement without enpowerment is responsibility without power. Power with responsibility entails both empowerment and engagement.

In the remainder of the book I will take these concepts as key points of reference. I will examine a number of debates that are central to building better cities: questions of rights and political participation, social welfare and economic arrangements. The titles of the next three chapters all share the word 'beyond', to denote a reordering of the conventional arguments of liberalism, welfarism and capitalism versus socialism in line with the guiding notions of encouraging empowerment and enhancing engagement. These are academic concepts and it is important to be familiar with the views of the key authors in each debate. This discussion, therefore, will move away from the generalizing slogan and concentrate on the phrasing of particularities. I sympathize with those distrustful or weary of such debates, and I will try to lighten the load of jargon and make the arguments more accessible. It is dangerous, however, to be dismissive of these academic discussions. 'Madmen in authority who hear voices in the air', wrote J. M. Keynes in 1936, 'are distilling their frenzy from some academic scribbler of a few years back.' Ideas have consequences, and consequences have consequences. Some ideas are just too important to be left to the academics.

6 Beyond Liberalism

... the most important point of excellence which any form of government can possess is to promote the virtue and intelligence of the people themselves. The first question in respect to any political institution is, how far they tend to foster in the members of the community the various desirable qualities, moral and intellectual ... The government which does this the best has every likelihood of being the best in all other respects.

J. S. Mill
Representative Government

Good cities are those which encourage the engagement of citizens in political discourse. The relationship between citizens and institutions of formal authority and political power has been dominated, at least in the west, for the last two hundred years by the influential discourse of liberalism. In this chapter I want to raise the issues of political engagement through an analysis of liberalism. I want to uncover its ideological basis to see if it is a secure foundation for our purposes.

Liberalism has two distinct meanings. It has been used to refer to a toleration of non-conformity, a willingness to encourage and protect diverse opinions and behaviours. This is traditional liberalism. Classical liberalism, in contrast, is a political philosophy stretching from Thomas Hobbes, through John Stuart Mill, to numerous contemporary writers. I will discuss the historical roots of classical liberalism and its influence on current debates through a brief examination of key writers, some more classic than others, and some less liberal than others.

Liberalism Defined: A Concern with Rights

Two early writers in the classical tradition are Thomas Hobbes (1588–1679) and John Locke (1632–1704). Both lived at a time when religious intolerance was being practised and absolutist power was being wielded. For Hobbes, the creation and maintenance of peace was the most important issue. For Locke, the key intellectual problem was how to maintain the rights of the individual, especially religious freedoms. As Protestants they could not draw upon the undisputed theology of the Catholic Church to provide morally sanctioned arguments. Nor was the divine right of kings an alternative. Both men were alive when a king had been executed and a republic had been declared in England in 1649. They responded to their problems with a contractual model of society in which individuals struck a bargain with the state. In Hobbes's view, because individuals could not trust one another, they should therefore give over their rights to one central authority which would then rule on their behalf. Without such authority, life would be 'solitary, poor, nasty, brutish and short'.

Locke used a similar contractual model but warned of the dangers of a state with great powers. If you could not trust your neighbour, as Hobbes had affirmed, how could you trust an all-powerful state? Locke believed that people had inalienable natural rights, and that the protection of these rights was the main task of government; the state was an instrument to enable individuals to pursue their legitimate ends and ultimate sovereignty lay with the people. Locke established the liberal tradition as we know it today. His main themes – society as discrete individuals with rights; the role of the state to ensure the rights of 'life, liberty and estate' – have continued to exercise the liberal mind and dominate the rhetoric, if sometimes not the practice, of western democracies.

Despite the difference in emphasis there are major similarities between Locke and Hobbes. Both shared a set of assumptions that Macpherson (1962) refers to as 'possessive individualism'. They viewed society as a set of property-owning individuals, and their concern was to provide the rules in which the property-holders could partake freely and benefit from economic transactions. Essentially they were concerned with the elaboration of

Plate 6.3 The Georgian New Town of Edinburgh was the physical expression of the Scottish Enlightenment, that flowering of ideas in the late eighteenth and early nineteenth centuries, which included the work of Adam Smith.

the rights of market man. In effect, they provided a philosophic rationale and political guide to the commercial bourgeoisie of seventeenth- and eighteenth-century England, at a time when it was beginning to emerge from the previous absolutist and feudal systems of obligation and authority.

Locke wrote a great deal about property and property rights. His position was a response to the charge that if God gave the land for all of humanity, there was no moral basis for individual claims to property. Locke's reply was to emphasize the exercise of human labour on land. Simple occupancy could not legitimate property rights; there had to be the pursuit and exercise of wealth-generating labour. The underlying assumption was that such labour improved on God's creation by increasing the level of material affluence in the society and thus benefiting other members of that society. His arguments were used against the claims of hunting–gathering societies in North America (who by merely enjoying the fruits of the land, were seen as failing to improve it) and have been used subsequently whenever commercial expansion meets traditional societies.

This defence of property had an implicit view of social welfare based on material wealth. Wealth-generating labour is seen as a legitimate basis of property rights, and this connection between individual gain and broader social purpose is hinted at in the common root shared by the terms 'property' and 'propriety'. Locke used the terms interchangeably in the early drafts of *Two Treatises of Government* first published in 1690.

Adam Smith (1723–90) published *The Wealth of Nations* in 1776, the same year as the American Declaration of Independence. Both events carried on the liberal tradition. Smith pointed to the limitations that should be placed on government if individual liberties are to be upheld. Smith codified the notion of a commercial society, and in particular the beneficial effects to society of the operation of the market. He who pursues private gain is, according to Smith: 'led by an invisible hand to promote an end which was no part of his intention. Nor is it always the worse for society that it was no part of it. By pursuing his own interest he frequently promotes that of society more effectually than when he really intends to promote it.' The invisible hand ties together private interests with the social good, thus obviating the need for an extensive state. Smith links political rights with

Plate 6.2 John Locke (1632–1704). © Mansell Collection.

Plate 6.1   Thomas Hobbes (1588–1679). © BBC Hulton Picture
Library.

the economic transactions of the market, maps out a restricted role for government and sees no distinction between individual and collective interests. He equates private ends with social progress.

The Debate Widened

The nineteenth century, first in Britain and then in other industrializing countries, saw the emergence of a working class, which did not own property and was thus excluded from the discourse of classical liberalism. It lacked property but it had economic muscle, a developing political power and a rhetoric that drew upon new-found class-consciousness and traditional peasant radicalism for the pursuit of equality and social justice. The working classes were important agents in the restructuring of capitalist societies. They used their power and influence to transform liberal states into liberal–democratic states. A new democratic veneer, including universal suffrage, was laid over older liberal concerns with the defence of property. Governments became involved in the operation of the market as the state was forced to exert its power and extend its role to achieve wider political goals. In response, liberalism became concerned with social justice as well as rights. The very concept of rights was extended, as in the slogan 'right to work', which employs the language of liberalism together with the demands of the unpropertied. Today, classical liberalism has two camps, those who argue for both rights and equality, and those who stress rights at the expense of equality.

Equality and Rights

The most influential work in this tradition is John Rawls's *A Theory of Justice* (1971). Rawls extends the concept of the social contract in considering what will best bind people together. He defines society as a 'cooperative venture for mutual advantage' and identifies the shared concept of justice as a binding mechanism because 'Among individuals with disparate aims and purposes a shared conception of justice establishes the bonds of civic friendship; the general desire for justice limits the pursuit of other ends. One may think of a public conception of justice as constituting the fundamental charter of a well-ordered human association'. The logical implication is that we need to develop principles of justice. In his model Rawls takes a group of rational people drawing up the ordering principles behind a veil of ignorance about their characteristics. These amnesiacs do not know if they are rich or poor, clever or ignorant, propertied or unpropertied. According to Rawls, this starting point will lead to principles that are fair to everyone, for if people know their position in society they might seek to establish principles that would favour their interests. From this position Rawls generates two key principles.

1   Each person is to have equal rights, e.g. the right to vote, freedom of thought, right to property etc.

2   Social and economic inequalities are tolerated only if they benefit the worst-off groups. Thus it would be fair to allow investors a 200 per cent increase in returns if the poor were to benefit from the action, say in terms of increased job opportunities.

The principles are ordered hierarchically. The first is the more fundamental. There can be no situation in which basic rights are to be sacrificed for increased prosperity. Rawls summarizes the position thus: 'All social values are to be distributed equally unless an unequal distribution of any, or all, of these values is to everyone's advantage' (62). Societies, institutions and cities ordered along these principles are defined as just.

Dworkin (1977) also seeks to defend liberalism from the criticisms that the emphasis on individual rights is merely a justification for those with property and ignores the fate of poorer groups in society. Dworkin, like Rawls, is a 'rights-plus-equality' liberal. Where Rawls connects questions of liberty and equality through two principles of justice, Dworkin conflates the two issues into one. Individual rights should be considered as trumps over the general good. Normally, considerations of general welfare will provide a reliable guide to social action and public policy. Thus, economic policies that raise average income would be preferred to policies which do not, but if some groups do not benefit, their economic rights are being transgressed. Policies that discriminate in their favour are thus to be preferred even though, consequently, general welfare may be lowered. In these special cases the individual rights override the concern with general welfare.

Classical Liberalism Revisited

While liberals such as Dworkin and Rawls seek to incorporate equality and put it on an equal footing with rights, others want to maintain rights at the expense of equality. Frederick Hayek is one of these 'rights-only' liberals. An anti-collectivist, he sees the pursuit of social justice as a mirage: 'the old civil rights and the new social and economic rights cannot be achieved at the same time but are in fact incompatible; the new rights could not be enforced by law without at the same time destroying that liberal order at which the civil rights aim' (1982, vol. 2, 103). In the 1940s and 1950s Hayek's ideas seemed quaint to most observers but in the 1970s and 1980s they have attracted powerful political allies seeking intellectual justification for the jettisoning of welfare programmes.

Another influential figure in this respect has been Nobel-prize-winning economist Milton Friedman. In *Free to Choose* (Friedman and Friedman, 1980) he resurrects Adam Smith's invisible hand of the market as the key to social welfare and economic progress. Economic success can be achieved and individual freedoms maintained, argues Friedman, only through a market free from government intervention, union power or public bureaucracies. The market knows best.

The philosopher Robert Nozick has also espoused arguments for a minimalist state. Anything more, he argued in *Anarchy, State and Utopia* (1974) would violate individual rights. Nozick levels his attack against the redistributional function of government. In order to achieve equality of holdings (income, property, etc.) governments have to keep interfering in order to achieve 'just' patterns of distribution. But patterned justice can only be achieved at the cost of constant and increasing government involvement. People are different and spend their holdings differently. He gives the example of a famous sportsman whom people will pay to see perform. Their actions will lead to an unequal distribution with the sportsman having more than others. To achieve patterned justice, the government must constantly violate people's right to property, and this results in an ever-meddling state. In contrast to the patterned theory, Nozick proposed an entitlement theory, which states that just distributions are those which occur when things are acquired justly. If the resources have been legally obtained then, according to Nozick, the state has no right to impose its redistributive function on individuals' holdings. The result is a minimal state, unviolated property rights and great inequality.

The 'new right' intellectuals of the 1970s and 1980s, such as Hayek, Friedman and Nozick, have laid claim to the traditional concerns of classical liberalism. They argue for the market and a minimalist state if individual rights (narrowly defined) are to be maintained and economic growth assured. They revive the arguments of Locke and Smith to combat increasing government intervention. Influential politicians and public figures have given their arguments wider currency, and so we are, in the words of F. Scott Fitzgerald, 'borne back ceaselessly into the past'.

The debate between the 'rights-only' and 'rights-plus-equality' strands of classical liberalism will continue. My preference lies with the Rawls and the Dworkins rather than the Hayeks and Nozicks. The latter define rights too narrowly and, to my mind, their desire for a minimal state will simply concentrate too much power in the corporate hands of the already-powerful, rich multinational companies, party political machines and, to a lesser extent, big unions. The argument for a minimal state in contemporary capitalist societies is, in effect, an intellectual justification for continued inequality of opportunity and outcome. I see a continued role for the state, but a role of enabling, of decentralizing, of giving more power to local communities. The state is an important factor in social change, and because it can be a vehicle for emancipation we ignore it at our peril.

Even though I disagree with the policy orientation and the political consequences of 'rights-only' liberalism, I find that some of its arguments cannot be easily dismissed. This strand of liberalism identifies concerns about individual rights and the encroaching power of the state, which refuse to disappear. Nozick, for example, raises important issues; even defenders of equality would benefit from reading his book.

The liberal debates are dominated by the private interests of individual property-owners and assume limited social obliga-

Plate 6.4   Free societies need dissidents. Debates about rights and obligations are too important to be left to the politicians. This graffiti in Reading, Berkshire, encourages us all to be critical participants.

tions. The urban world we live in, however, is one where we live together and where our actions have repercussions on others; where the rights of some can be translated into the hardships of others. The city is a place where our public and private lives merge, and where our individual and social selves cannot easily be separated. Such places extend the terms of the liberal debate. We need to go beyond liberalism because in cities there is more to public life, government and democracy than the protection of individual property rights.

Beyond Liberalism: Encouraging the Civic Tradition

I hesitate to use the term 'beyond liberalism'. Individual rights are important and we must fight to get basic rights of life, liberty and justice established and extended around the world. Classical liberalism has been concerned with the dangers of state power encroaching on the rights of individuals and, thus, has provided an intellectual bulwark against the use of arbitrary state power. Liberal arguments have been made appealing when contrasted with Marxism and associated forms of centralized socialism where too much power has been given to the state. My argument is not that rights are unimportant, rather that they can only be achieved in a social context; it is this context that we must now examine.

The problem with liberalism is the failure to assemble its rights-orientated individuals into a purposeful society. If people are all pursuing their own ends, how can they combine to reach agreement about wider social goals, such as the creation of more humane cities, let alone achieve them? The market fulfilled this role for Locke and Smith and, more recently, for Friedman and Hayek. Markets do have important functions in coordinating decisions, channelling actions and giving power to consumers, but they have too many divisive and regressive effects to be the sole device for social integration. The quote by Smith cited on p. 83 only says that the pursuit of self-interest 'frequently' promotes that of society, it does not say that it 'always', 'in a majority of cases' or even 'necessarily' does. Even for the father of free market economics then, the market system does not automatically lead to the best social outcomes.

Classical liberalism lacks a convincing argument about the connection between individual and collective interests and says very little about that space between individual rights and state power in which we find much of the life of a city and its citizens. This area is the subject of another tradition in political philosophy, whose roots lie as far back as Aristotle and which extends through Rousseau, Hegel and Marx to such twentieth-century writers as R. H. Tawney, Hannah Arendt and Michael Walzer. The writers of what I will term the 'civic tradition', share a number of characteristics. In contrast to the unencumbered, atomized individuals of classical liberalism, they see people as essentially political beings whose individual capacities are fully realized only in the discussion and pursuit of collective goals. The failure of individuals to achieve this engagement, this sense of social purpose, is one definition of alienation. From this perspective, classical liberalism is seen at best as an impoverished theory concentrating on private rights and not on the private–public set of rights and obligations and, at worst, as a justification for the continued inequalities of market society.

The civic tradition has a very different model of the political process. In contrast to classical liberalism it stresses participation and engagement and shares the anarchist fear of a powerful state. In both Aristotle and Rousseau, we read that citizens should take turns at holding administrative tasks. The concept of a permanent bureaucracy is a worrying one for the civics.

The civic tradition has much to recommend it. The emphasis on participation chimes with the themes of empowerment and engagement. The problem is how we can promote the civic tradition in a way that is responsive to liberty and rights – not simply the right of property, as in Nozick, or the market liberties of Friedman, but rights and liberties that ensure an equal opportunity to develop individual potential. A lot depends on the details of government structure. I will develop this theme with reference to forms of urban government, but first let me deal briefly with the anarchist challenge.

The Anarchist Challenge

Any defence of formal government must respond to the anarchist challenge that all formal government is an imposition on our freedom. As early as 1793 William Goodwin, in his *Enquiry Concerning Political Justice*, was criticizing government for its failure to promote the general good and its use of systematic oppression in the name of law and order. Richard Sennett's *The Uses of Disorder* (1970) provides a modern treatment of the anarchist theme applied to urban communities. His prescription for self-policing communities could herald some form of internal dialogue between the various groups rather than a reliance on external coercion. Sennett provides a fascinating glimpse of a truly alternative city. His book needs to be on all urban studies courses because it questions many of our assumptions and, if we care to listen, may shake our beliefs.

Plate 6.5 This banner in a demonstration in Barcelona, Spain, expresses the essential anarchist distaste for the state.

During the twentieth century the central state has accumulated enormous power. This has often been for the very best of reasons: at the behest of radical groups and reforming movements seeking to improve social conditions, the state has been charged with ensuring minimum standards of health provision, wage levels and a host of other programmes. Some states have been more successful than others but the general trend, and one which should not be lightly dismissed, has been an increase in the quality of material life. The new deals, great societies, welfare states and other national welfare programmes have improved the life chances of many, but at a price. Power has been concentrated in distant centres, less-deserving groups have also benefited from state actions, sometimes more so than the intended beneficiaries, and there have been many costly failures. We can identify a number of laws for administrative blunders: anything that can go wrong will go wrong; most public policies will achieve half of what they promise and cost twice as much as they initially forecast; expensive bureaucracies live on long after their programmes have achieved their goals; the sharp elbows of the middle class will make sure that they benefit most from universal benefits such as free education and health.

To take as much power as possible away from the state in the long term is a desirable goal; perhaps the demise of the state will be a mark of our social progress. In the short term, however, the state exists and needs to be used by people of good will, otherwise it will only be used by people of bad. The state is not the only route to social improvement: small-scale initiatives that build on the creativity of local responses can also achieve much. However, because it is there, the state remains an important route for deliberate, organized social change and the pursuit of greater empowerment.

Forms of Government

If we accept that there is a role for formal government, then what is the most appropriate form to enhance empowerment and engagement? My basic answer is to make the centres of state power more accessible and responsive. Government should be visible, immediate and accessible, and this involves shifting the locus of state power from centralized systems towards more local centres responsible for the bulk of taxing and spending.

There are two models of state structure. The dominant one is the top-down, 'central–local' system, which concentrates power in the centre, requires a centralized bureaucracy and concedes limited autonomy to local governments. In the alternative bottom-up, 'local–central' system, power is diffused among a number of small-scale local governments and the role of the central authority is more limited. A necessary step toward the empowerment of individual citizens thus involves a shift from a central–local to a local–central form of government, because such a change involves a decentralization of power and the curtailment of the power of centralized bureaucracies and corporate interests. A larger number of smaller power centres would make it more difficult for corporate interests to influence government.

The central–local model has dominated the political life of advanced democracies (with some notable exceptions, such as Switzerland) and has forced a narrow definition of political culture:

> Those who look from the top down consider that the whole authority of the state is concentrated at the centre. To them, the centre is the only legitimate source of power: it is from the central government that local authorities receive their powers: indeed the central government actually creates the local authorities, dividing up the state into more or less uniform divisions in the process . . .
> The central government does this for the more efficient and economic provision of its services. It involves the leading citizens of every locality in the business of government, not so much in order to hear their views, as in order to embrace them and make them identify themselves with the system. This school of thought . . . is more interested in efficiency than in democracy, in uniform standards than in local responsibility; it regards the citizen more as consumer of services than participant in government. Even at its best, it is apt to be patronising. (Rees, 1971)

There are two paradoxes for the average citizen in this form of government: the most accessible forms of government are the least effective, and the most powerful politicians are those with whom they have least contact. An appropriate local–central form would seek to reverse this situation by linking accessibility with power, and by connecting politicians more closely to the lives of their representatives.

The centralization of politics has meant single power centres, accessible to the big and powerful. The ordinary citizen would have difficulty finding his or her way around the complicated bureaucracies of Whitehall or Washington, whereas multinationals, in contrast, have the influence and money to capture the ear of government. Individual citizens are alienated from the power that governs much of their lives. We have become disconnected from the fabric of our political culture, bystanders in the political life of our countries, our connection too often little more than a general election every four to five years. A change in the form of government would not overcome the feelings of apathy, but a change from central–local to local–central would be a move in

Plate 6.6   City Hall in Los Angeles, USA, is a proud symbol of city government. Throughout the world such local governments are under threat from increasingly powerful central governments. Is local urban government feasible? Can it be equitable, efficient and democratic?

the right direction. More localized forms of government provide greater possibilities for citizen engagement because smaller-scale, more localized units of government would allow greater contact between the representatives and the represented. As Lewis Mumford noted:

> For democracy, in any active sense, begins and ends in communities small enough for their members to meet face to face. Without such units, capable of independent and autonomous action, even the best-contrived central governments, state or federal, become party-orientated, indifferent to criticism, resentful of correction, and in the end, all too often, high-handed and dictatorial. (1968, 224)

What should be the most appropriate size for our local authorities? Too large and they replicate the problems of the centralized system; too small and they could experience the problems found by many urban governments in the USA, where metropolitan fragmentation of government allows some richer communities to keep out the poor and ethnic minorities. This leads to a fiscal disparity between the poorer, inner-city municipalities, which have limited financial resources but high needs, and the richer, suburban communities, which have a healthier tax base but fewer demands. This problem could be avoided by a division of municipalities, which would maximize social heterogeneity without compromising political accessibility. It is surely not beyond our abilities to identify an optimum range of sizes that achieves this goal.

We could begin to think of governments for city regions including not just the city centre, but the suburbs and outlying rural districts, with boundaries based on contemporary communting and shopping patterns, labour markets and historical allegiance. Units of government must be meaningful, connected with the lives of citizens, not arbitrary lines on a map. A useful subdivision within these city regions could be local school districts. Not only would this provide a focus for adult attention but would also provide a point of contact between children and the wider society. Lessons could be arranged around the discovery of the local community and the construction of a community profile along the lines of:

constructing and updating maps of the district;

constructing a profile – basic distribution and age, gender, ethnicity, etc., and discovering the different histories of the local population;

regular monitoring of community preferences and needs through questionnaires;

regular monitoring of the wide forces affecting the district, e.g. surveys of changing markets for local industries;

regular surveys of local political issues, providing forums for debate and allowing alternative voices to be heard.

When schools are used to take the pulse of the community then children are given an education about their own society, which is neither parochial nor unconnected to the lives and experiences of their parents. We rarely involve children in political debates. If we fail to do so it is no wonder we produce political apathetics. The schools should be a centre of debate about community needs and political means and ends. Too much school work is unrelated to the direct experience of children, their parents and their community. By making the school district not only a unit of government but an important centre for data collection and debate we reconnect education and experience, children and adults, civil and political society.

There is a need for representative democracy. Even in smaller units of government there is likely to be a need for a set of elected officials. However, the local–central alternative discussed here assumes an active citizenry, which 'places the emphasis on local authorities as nurseries of democratic citizenship, revels in diversity and local initiative, is impatient of central control and wishes to involve the citizen, not so much to bring him [and her] into contract with the state, as to foster his [and her] self-reliance' (Rees, 1971). To this end we can think less of a simple three-to-four-year election turnout and more of a continual interaction between people and the state. A certain number of positions on any council should be set aside for citizen involvement on the same basis as for jury service, that is, as a civic right and

Plate 6.7 Children turn spaces into places. This school playground in Canberra, Australia, is enlivened by children; the same could be done for civic debates.

obligation open to all. Few people find jury service irksome – in fact most feel that they are fulfilling a worthwhile duty. The same system could be gradually incorporated into representative forms of government so that everyone gets a turn, every citizen has the right and the obligation to perform in a governmental institution whether it be alongside or as replacement for elected representatives.

If there is a need for elected representatives their tenure should be limited to a certain specified period, perhaps four to five years. Just as there is a statutory limit on presidential terms of office so should local politicians be kept from continual representation. Long-term tenure of political office is unhealthy for the incumbent and the office. Regular elections, automatic recall with a majority referendum, pegging politicians' expenses so that they receive the average wage in the area and limitations on the length of service are just some of the methods possible to bring the governing closer to the governed, to make sure that those who represent us do not become too distant from us.

Respecting people's rights also means respecting the rights of the politically inactive, the disengaged, those with too few evenings to spare. There is a need for a form of ombudsman to whom people can appeal for help or assistance. A system that enables ordinary citizens to inquire into the system of local government itself is also an initial requirement, so as to minimize the possibility that the local state may be captured by local elites and used to further their particular sectional goals. The pro-development lobby of many local authorities is often a means of self-enrichment at the cost of wider community interests. This is not a fault of local government but of the current form of local government, which lacks power and fails to attract the interest of the local population. If the local government had much more power people would begin to take much more notice, activists would have an interest in staying in the local area and minority groups concerned simply with lining their own pockets would have a much harder time.

Ultimately, the most effective way to shift power from the central to the local state is to transfer primary responsibility for taxation and spending. The local authority would raise revenue through property and income taxes and be the major spender for public goods and services. There would still be a role for a central authority, but its function would be restricted to hearing appeals, acting as arbiter in disputes between different local states, and providing a small number of goods and services that could not be supplied by local authorities. So-called 'pure' public goods, such as lighthouses or defence, would be included in this category. The central authority could also pool a certain amount of local-state revenue and redistribute it to equalize the spending abilities of the diverse local authorities. The pool should be small to discourage too much control passing to the central authorities, but large enough to allow local authorities to draw upon the central fund to meet legitimate but unforeseen needs, for example to provide a relief fund for natural disasters. A scheme could be devised, perhaps based on Rawlsian principles.

A federation of local authorities would pose special problems. There is evidence of some authorities being more willing than national governments to sacrifice long-term environmental quality for short-term economic gains. To ensure that local authorities do not sacrifice precious resources for short-term advantage, some form of second chamber elected for longer periods may be appropriate. A local–central system also creates difficulties for central coordination of services; however, this might be no bad thing. No longer would local communities have to face constant impositions in 'the national interest' or for 'reasons of state'. Limits would be placed on the power of nation-states, and in an era of nuclear weaponry this is an important issue. The more that state authorities can centralize power, the easier it is for them to speak for a national interest that is not shared by a significant proportion of the population. Thus, it would be difficult for a central authority to pursue a defence policy (though this seems a strange name for strategies of mass destruction and death) if many of the local authorities were to refuse to pay for such 'defence' expenditure.

A local–central system would offer a diversity of public policies and, assuming free movement, people would have a significant measure of choice. It is easy to imagine how different local authorities, building on and reflecting local traditions and cultures, could express a range of political and economic arrangements, from controlled economies, through the varieties of mixed economies, to the kinds of anarchic urban community proposed by Richard Sennett. Despite the many difficulties, the local–

central arrangement would allow us to maximize choice and enhance engagement.

Alternative Power Centres

We should be careful not to restrict our notions of political engagement and empowerment to the formal arena of politics. Of course it is important to get better formal arrangements, but it is just as important to make sure that ordinary citizens have a role in the exercise of power involved outside of the debating chamber. Of the many possible areas let me discuss just two.

Public Services

The state provides a whole variety of goods and services. For those services which are collectively consumed, such as public transport, there is a need for both worker and consumer representation on the management boards. As we have already noted in chapter 4, not all citizens are given enough institutional room to express their particular needs, especially if they are not middle-aged, middle-income, car-owning men. User groups do exist, but we need to improve them. This could be achieved in two main ways: first, by giving workers and users statutory rights in the running of public organizations; second, by ensuring a wide coverage in the worker and user representation. The British reliance on the select band of the great and the good ensures that the middle-income voice is consistently heard, but rarely allows a hearing to anyone else. We need a continual input of fresh blood by restricting participation to just one board and for a restricted period. A careful phasing of representation should ensure change and stability. If every member were to vacate their place on the board after four years, but out of ten members only two were replaced each year this would have the advantage of allowing a continual input of new people whilst maintaining a constant pool of expertise. Members of the management board of an urban public transport authority, for example, should include equal representation of workers, management and users. The consumer representation should include actual users such as teenagers, old persons, people looking after children, those using public transport mainly to get to and from work and those who rely upon it for shopping. Such a set-up may not cure the transport problems of the city, but it will ensure that more than just the car-owning, white males will have their interests represented.

Where goods are provided publicly but are consumed individually, such as public housing, there is much greater scope for self-management schemes. Examples of such schemes in North America and Britain have had varying degrees of success, depending on the level of community involvement and resource provision. Self-management is often used at the same time as provision of resources is cut back. The management of declining expenditure and rising demands is a difficult context. At its best, self-management of public housing projects has allowed local people to exercise care and attention and exhibit pride in their neighbourhood. At its worst, the schemes have run into difficulty over general issues, such as the level of wider community involvement and particulars such as the allocation of vacant property to needy families who fail to meet community standards. On the whole, allowing tenants to control the when, where and how of housing maintenance and allocation is one way of empowering and engaging people previously treated as recipients of decisions made by others. This engagement has many positive benefits in terms of reducing vandalism and maintenance costs and allowing new forms of self- and community-expression in areas previously marked by a drab uniformity.

Urban Design and Planning

There are some areas so important that community involvement is vital. The argument of chapter 2 is that urban design and planning is too important to be left to the professionals.

In terms of urban planning, the community needs to be involved at the two stages of plan formulation and plan implementation. In Britain, ever since the Town and Country Planning Act of 1968, planning authorities have a statutory duty to run public participation schemes at the plan-formulation stage. The involvement is generally low and restricted to the better-organized pressure groups. There is nothing inherently wrong with this – the others may not be concerned, or may have too little time to spare. I have a lingering feeling, however, that not everyone finds out about the schemes. Using schools as places of debate and schoolchildren as a participative audience is one way of increasing the range of input.

'Plan formulation' is too vague a term and a concept for the general public to appreciate. It is couched in a technical language and assumes an ability with maps that is not shared by everyone. Plan preparation, therefore, is not an obvious point of contact with the everyday lives of people, who are likely to be interested not in five-year plans but in the impact of a particular building on a specific site. At this level of planning implementation the British system has no obligation to ensure public participation. It should have. The decision-making over the shape, size and location of buildings is a matter of public importance and open to interested members of the community. All projects above a certain height or floorspace size and even smaller projects in sensitive areas, should be widely advertised and opportunities given for community groups to make representation. This involves holding planning committee meetings at convenient times and with enough facilities for easy access and crèches to allow the participation of the disabled and those looking after children.

Too many building designs are imposed on the users without any consultation. Public participation needs to be extended to the internal design as well as the external structure. Formal planning in Britain, as elsewhere, is dominated by the outsides of buildings, and not their internal design.

At present there is a pro-development bias. Ranged against rich interest groups, local communities often have too little power. One small improvement would be to introduce social impact analysis (SIA), funded by the developers and organized by an independent body for all large to medium building proposals. These SIAs should be written in a non-technical, accessible language, perhaps in a standard format, and should include a socially sensitive cost–benefit analysis. The reports should be freely distributed and could be a point of discussion in the local school. Other improvements could be the funding of objections to major planning proposals paid for from development charges so that poor community groups are not denied access and the right of appeal to objectors when the decision allows development. In Britain at present, appeals are only possible when development is rejected.

Plate 6.8 Civic design should incorporate our need for places to sit down and take it easy for a while. Here is a good example from Greenwich Village, in Manhattan, USA.

Developers are canny people, sensitive to local conditions. The point is to change these conditions, to change the climate of opinion so that developers have to construct pleasant, usable buildings in well-integrated neighbourhoods. We can reclaim aesthetic and political control of our cities, and still give the developers freedom to work and make money.

The public life of a city is only as good as the public life of its citizens. By ensuring engagement and enhancing empowerment we open up the possibilities of greater citizen involvement, greater civic responsibility and greater civic pride.

7 Beyond Welfarism

> A vital new debate is beginning, or perhaps an old debate is being renewed, about the proper role of government, the welfare state and the attitudes on which it rests. Many of the issues at stake have been debated on countless occasions in the last century or two. Some are as old as philosophy itself.
>
> Margaret Thatcher
> *Collected Speeches*

Some goods and services can be provided on the basis of need or demand rather than the ability to pay. I will use the term 'welfarism' to describe their provision. In most rich cities elements of health, education, housing and transport are provided in this way. The provision of such goods is an important element of the humane city. But legitimate questions arise about the limits of the provision (for example, should education be provided in this fashion or not? Is there a role for public housing?). We can also question the precise mechanism of provision and payment (Should students of higher education be given grants or loans? What is a fair rent for public housing?). These are important issues but I will not discuss them here. Rather, I want to look at the ideological legacy of welfarism; I want to see how our present debates have their roots in the past, before I make a few remarks about the limits and provision of welfare items.

Countries vary in the extent and quality of welfare provision. We can distinguish at least three different types: the *residual* (for example the USA and Australia), where the greatest benefits go to the employed and there is a form of means-testing for the poor; the *institutional* (for example the UK), which involves a national minimum standard while allowing the wealthier to buy better education and health; and the *universal* (for example Sweden), which involves a maximization of collective welfare. The comments in this chapter are drawn from the experience of the second type, although they are of relevance to them all.

Although there had been social pressures and administrative responses in the nineteenth and early twentieth centuries, the real moment for welfarism came in the post-1945 period, when most rich capitalist countries were forced by popular pressure to develop welfare programmes. The transformation of WARFARE/welfare states into WARFARE/WELFARE states represents one of the biggest social changes of the twentieth century.

One strand of welfarism developed out of the charities of the nineteenth century. These institutions, public and private, sought to provide relief from poverty. They were motivated by philanthropy, theology and a fear of social unrest. There were too many poor people for their limited means and so the charitable institutions rationed their resources. Their customers were made recipients and told to wait in line for the handout. The charities made a distinction between the deserving and undeserving poor. The deserving were those who were poor through no fault of their own, the undeserving were the 'bone idle', that is, those unwilling to work; one was a legitimate cause for concern, the other a social leech to be denied support. The images of the needy widow and the lazy scrounger condensed the distinction. The charitable basis continues in the language of contemporary welfare, with its welfare 'recipients' and the 'needy'. This is in contrast to the language we use for private consumption – the terms 'consumer sovereignty' and 'free choice', for example, conjure up images of free people making choices. Welfarism has its legacy in language as well as in its tradition of queuing, suffering and rationing.

Another strand in contemporary welfarism, again related to its ideological inheritance, is the way goods and services are provided in a top-down manner. Major decisions are frequently taken by senior bureaucrats with little or no consultation or participation. The flow of decision-making and the locus of power reinforces the notion of welfarism as philanthropy in which the recipients of 'charity' must dutifully accept the decisions of those who 'know best'.

There are now some areas where the recipients see themselves as consumers. Welfare facilities that are heavily used by articulate groups, such as education, are now seen more as a right than a privilege. Increasing expectations and the growing articulateness of all groups, but especially the middle-income groups, are producing welfare 'consumers' who are not satisfied with the top-down, charity mentality of much welfare provision. For them, welfare services are a right not a favour to be appreciated. This is not the case where consumers are predominantly lower-income, less-articulate groups. In public housing, for example, notions of charity and privileges are still entrenched. It is as if the provision of public goods and services that benefit the worse-off members of society are welfare benefits, while those that benefit the rest of society are rights. This is the old distinction between the deserving and undeserving poor in a new guise, and it becomes a major issue during fiscal crunches because it is easier to reduce spending on the 'undeserving'. The case of housing finance in Britain will illustrate this. Benefits to owner-occupiers amounted to £5000 million in 1981–2, while benefits to public-housing tenants came to around £350 million. Government spending cutbacks of 1983–4 sliced over 50 per cent from subsidies to public housing, which was stigmatized as 'welfare benefits', but subsidies to owner-occupation were untouched.

Welfarism Questioned

The commitment to welfarism, strong in the 1950s and 1960s, is now being questioned by a range of interests. The main reason is the crisis in funding. Many governments now face the problem of constant or increasing expenditure with declining or static revenue. This problem has been particularly acute in the welfare sector because:

> People now expect and demand more from the state than their parents did or their grandparents ever imagined. Expectations once raised are politically difficult to reduce. Increases in demand have also occurred due to demographic changes. The ageing of national populations, for example, puts a strain on welfare provision in countries where the care of the elderly is more of a public obligation than a family duty;

Plate 7.1   Public housing in Glasgow: welfare for the poor?

The welfare sector is very labour intensive. Other sectors of the economy can reduce costs by shedding labour, making the welfare sector more expensive in comparative terms: this is referred to as the 'relative price effect';

There are entrenched interests in the welfare sector. Trade unions and professional groups continually lobby governments to spend more money.

Plate 7.2   Owner-occupation in Sussex: welfare for the middle incomes?

Plate 7.3   Entrance to the Clore Gallery at the Tate, London: welfare for the intelligentsia?

The limits to government expenditure are ultimately set by taxpayers, both individual and corporate. The creation of a WARFARE/WELFARE state was based on a widening and deepening tax base. The 1970s and 1980s have seen revolts at both local and national levels against perceived increases in the tax burden. Particularly vocal have been the middle-income groups, who see themselves as the milch cows for a burgeoning welfare bureaucracy designed to help the lower-income groups. The ideology of individualism, particularly strong in the middle-classes, clashes with the practice of redistributional taxation.

The financial constraints have led to a re-examination of the welfare system. The Right have questioned the usefulness of welfare expenditure, arguing that it reflects the power of welfare bureaucrats more than the needs of the poor. They also employ the spectre of the undeserving poor, the welfare scroungers. The works of old critics of welfarism, such as Hayek, have been brought down from the shelves, the dust blown off and their arguments repeated. The anti-welfare arguments have gained some ground. At a popular level there has been increasing disquiet with the quality of many public services and the Right has successfully appealed to many wage- and salary-earners whose taxes pay for welfarism. The response of the Left has been more complex. From the mid-1960s and the rediscovery of poverty through to the 1970s there was a feeling that the welfare state had not improved the relative position of the worst-off. Evidence has been gathered to show the disproportionate benefits obtained by the middle-income groups (see Le Grand, 1982). These criticisms have tended to evaporate in the face of attacks on welfarism. Many on the Left have felt it necessary to defend the welfare state, and there is much to be defended. Yet apart from supporting the vague notion of shifting resources from warfare to welfare there have been few fundamental re-examinations of the costs, benefits and consequences of welfarism in contemporary society. While the Right has mounted a powerful case for social policy to be shaped by fiscal 'realities' the Left, in defending welfarism from attack, has mainly been locked into an uncritical defence of the welfare sector.

Beyond Welfarism: Encouraging a Caring City

A caring society is one where people need not lose their dignity if they are ill or fall on hard times or simply grow old; where each child is encouraged to fulfil his or her own potential and develop his or her talents; and where people can live like human beings. The humane city is the built form of the caring society.

The debates on welfarism have polarized into either cutting or defending welfare. In the rest of this chapter I want to go beyond this dichotomy to consider how we can combine the resources of a centralized system with the sensitivity of a local one. I will restrict my comments to health although the broad arguments apply to education and housing.

Collective Provision

There are many valid arguments for the collective provision of health. Few of us have the resources to pay for unforeseen medical bills. By joining together, either in a public or a private arrangement, we pool our resources. There is also an insurance element. We may be healthy and relatively rich in our youth and middle-age, yet old age may bring long-term illness for ourselves or our family. By subscribing to a collective health provision scheme we insure ourselves and our families from future misfortunes.

The question then arises – public or private? A universal public scheme has the advantage of wide coverage. The more individual contributions there are, the more resources are available to any individual patient. The system needs to be as universal as possible. Private schemes can deal with short-term illness, but they do not have the resources to deal with the long-term ill, the infirm and all those requiring constant care over very long periods. Private schemes do not provide solutions for all citizens and thus cannot provide the only health care that a caring city needs. Only a universal public health scheme can do this. However, there are different types of public health care. The state can lay down certain standards of health care, but it does not have to become involved in its actual provision.

Individual Consumption

One reason for the growth of private health schemes is the belief amongst those who can afford it that they will get a better
service, and in this they have a point. Collective provision can all
too easily be translated into collective consumption, where patients are treated simply as the recipients of a health-care delivery
system designed to suit the bureaucrats and the professionals. To
enter a large National Health Service hospital in Britain can
make you feel as though you are a character in a Kafka novel:
the bureaucratic procedures have a life of their own; people come
and go, doctors arrive and leave, and you sense that you do not
amount to very much. This feeling is not due to the personnel –
there are marvellous nurses and good doctors – but to the system
itself, which seems to operate on an impersonal basis so that
'patients' receive treatment, but 'individuals' do not receive care
and attention.

The pivotal point of any health-care system is the dignity of the
patient: this above all should be the guiding principle, the ultimate criterion, which guides choices and decisions. At present,
the health services are dominated by the medical profession.
There is asymmetrical power in the doctor–patient relationship,
which needs to be put on a more equal footing. There is a need
for a bill of rights for patients, which would stress the sovereignty of choice concerning doctor and treatment. We could
make a good start by making a doctor's education more responsive to human needs. To pass a medical degree you need memory,
raw intelligence and hard work. Doctors need more training in
communication and basic counselling skills as well as medical
literacy.

The medical profession as a whole is arrogant and mindful of
its power, stressing science and technology rather than care and
love. But we cannot lay all the blame on the medics: most
patients have given up control of their own health to professionals. The doctor–patient power asymmetry is maintained by the
dominant image of ill health as something we 'get' and the belief
that we need doctors to get rid of 'it'. The alternative view
regards ill health not as something we get, but as the way we are.
'Disease' means exactly what it says: 'dis-ease', an imbalance in

Plate 7.4   The collective provision of open space is an important
component of any civilized city: Central Park, New York, USA.

our lives. We can cure many diseases not by drugs but by changing life-styles and attitudes. Ill health has a social function. When
a child gets ill, it may receive care. If this is the only time it
receives such attention, the child may encourage further attention
by continuing to be ill or have recurring illness. A great deal
needs to be done, and can be done quite cheaply, about the
social-psychological basis of illness. At the moment we are
dominated by the notion of illness 'out there', and of ourselves as
passive receivers of illness. We do have control and power over
our bodies yet our health system gives over most of the responsibility to others.

   In a caring city there is a need for a public health service dominated by the need to secure and maintain the dignity of patients. One organizational change to the present system would be to encourage much smaller, more local hospitals. The tendency for the size of hospitals to increase may be a bureaucratic convenience, but it distances patients from personal medical care. The sheer scale of many modern hospitals is discouraging and alienating to most patients. Well-run, smaller hospitals bring health care down to a more personal, more accessible scale. These hospitals need not be arms of the central state. Alternative forms of provision involving combinations of local business, medical workers, cooperatives and community groups could, with minimum standards laid down, become more accessible forms of health-care delivery.

Health care should be about maintaining health. The small-scale hospitals should be as concerned with health as they are currently concerned with disease. Local hospitals should be centres for education in the local community informing people about the importance of diet and life-style. Equally important is the need for hospitals to be part of the local community, to be involved in local issues of health, such as housing standards, lead levels and pollution, and to be concerned with what is happening in local workplaces. Contemporary medical centres are unconnected with local communities and ignorant, at an institutional level, of the nature of people's work and lives. Modern medicine seems concerned only with the ill health of people. To be effective in preventing disease medical centres must connect more with local communities.

The overriding concern with ill health means that hospitals are primarily concerned with treating the ill. Perhaps we could experiment with the Community Health Organizations found in North America where the onus is on the centre to avoid its patients falling ill. People sign up with the CHOs and pay a standard charge, and if they become ill or require treatment there are no more charges. The CHOs thus benefit if people stay healthy. There is a danger of unscrupulous doctors refusing to give treatment to people who need it, but if the CHO experiment can be tried in a modified form in a public health system this problem may be overcome. The present system needs to be changed as it is just too expensive.

A more basic system to keep people healthy could be devised. What we need is a change in basic attitudes towards health and disease and towards treatment. The drug companies and the medical profession have together managed to make treatment dependent on expensive drugs and equipment. If we were to concentrate attention on self-healing and life-style changes then much of the medical cost would disappear. There would still be a place for the use of drugs, but on a more reduced scale. Changing attitudes and making hospitals more locally responsible and funded, with some sort of resource-equalization scheme in operation, and with limits on expenditure, would focus attention on keeping people healthy rather than waiting for them to get ill. User-friendly, smaller-scale, community-connected, health-promoting rather than illness-caring, medical centres would seem to be a cheaper, more effective form of health care.

If we have a commitment to basic principles of welfarism, and I believe good caring cities need a welfare element, then we must go beyond the sterile argument of whether to dismantle or defend the welfare state. It is not good enough to say, 'Let us save the welfare system and then reform it later'. Present circumstances allow us to defend but also go beyond welfarism.

In terms of defence, we need a much broader examination of the costs and benefits not only of *providing* but also of *not providing* welfare goods and services. The cost and benefits of alternative types of provision also warrant special consideration. For example, a comparison between a health system concerned more with basic preventative health care than the high-tech solutions for those already ill may widen and enlighten the welfare debate. We need to provide measurements beyond simplified costs and narrow benefits and to open up the debate beyond the present circumscribed limits set by notions of administrative efficiency, monetarist ideologies and philanthropic notions of 'charity'.

In terms of going beyond contemporary welfarism, we need to move from a top-down towards a more bottom-up system in which user preferences, subject to budget restraints, are paramount. Effective consumer participation is necessary to make the provision of welfare goods and services more responsive to changing public needs and aspirations, and less subject to the influence of the various professional groups involved. There is not enough decentralization of decision-making. Powerful senior administrators may know the broad outline of public demand, but they are frequently insensitive to the finer scale of public preferences: witness the now-empty high-rise public-housing blocks in Britain and America once favoured by public-housing administrators but now abandoned by consumers. In the 1960s and early 1970s public-housing schemes were dominated by high-rise solutions in which existing neighbourhoods were cleared and people rehoused in tower blocks. These blocks were promoted by the builders and their friends in government, the architectural profession and civic authorities. By almost everyone in fact except the people who had to live in them. The future tenants were not consulted, and the end result was a notoriously unpopular form of housing.

In the case of the British National Health Service, although all health workers have some power (for example unskilled workers can cause havoc by striking) only doctors, and particularly the senior consultants, can influence the basic direction of health care. Their priorities are patterned into the very structure of the health service. It would be strange if it were otherwise. However, because of the top-down decision-making and the enduring legacy of 'experts-know-best' and the ideology of 'these-are-benefits-not-rights', there is only a limited counterweight to established medical power. A wide disparity exists between the senior medics who 'man' the system and the consumers. Senior consultants are invariably middle- to upper-income men; they have much power, yet their life experience, ethnicity, gender and class rarely correspond with the mass of consumers. Women, and working-class women in particular, have a difficult time with an insensitive system in which they have little say and no power. The result is a health system that reflects medical power more than consumer needs.

Changing the welfare system to one that is more open, with community involvement and decentralization of power, will not solve all the problems. There will still be conflicting demands from different sectors of the community and budget constraints will continue to exist. But a system with an empowered and engaged set of consumers and producers will encourage alternative views to those of the dominant professional groups. It could make welfare facilities much more responsive to consumer needs.

To date, the efficiency of consumer sovereignty has only been theorized with reference to the private market. We need to enshrine it as a guiding principle in the public domain. It will not be a panacea, but as an important element for creating better cities, it could be cheaper and it would certainly be fairer.

8 Beyond Capitalism versus Socialism

The intelligent radical keeps his head; he argues the virtues of the free market when the tendency is to think only of the need for particular interventions, and he stresses the need for social interventions whenever laissez-faire becomes an object of religious devotion.

James Meade
The Intelligent Radical's Guide To Economic Policy

The last two hundred years have seen the strengthening of the capitalist mode of production. This has involved the deepening and extending of the calculus of profitability, a growing concern with exchange values rather than use values and the development of production according to market signals. The enthronement of capitalism has not been uncontested. Within capitalist countries there have been struggles around the points of material and cultural production, and, elsewhere in the world, revolutionary movements have replaced market capitalism with either state capitalism or state socialism.

The 'capitalist versus socialist' division is now the major ideological cleavage in the world community and the dominant opposition in political discourse. Other voices, such as those of anarchists and syndicalists, have been raised against capitalism, but they have not achieved the prominence or the success of the socialists. A variety of groups cluster under the socialist banner, from reformist social democrats to revolutionaries, but there is enough coherence, in principle if not in practice, to speak of a broad socialist challenge to the capitalist ethic.

The Debate

Ideas reflect the process of contestation. Like combatants in a ring, they position themselves with reference to their opponents. The socialist challenge has been defined primarily with reference to capitalism. The traditional socialist challenge to the capitalist order derives more from the experience of capitalism than a fully articulated rival set of beliefs. The traditional lines of the capitalist-versus-socialist debate: the desire to replace the anarchy of the market with a planned economy, the goal of reducing inequalities seemingly inherent in the operation of the market, and the need to take private industry into public ownership, are important but not all that helpful in thinking about cities as if people matter. Major questions of empowerment and engagement are ignored.

A biographical note may be of some assistance to the reader. I was born and raised in a small mining village in Scotland. The place had a population of about 5,000 – including my extended family of ten aunts and uncles and over forty cousins. I was given a profoundly socialist informal education. This background and experience meant that I could not accept the top-down Fabianism which often passes for socialism in Britain whereby intellectuals 'give' socialism to the masses. Perhaps I was oversensitive, but I could detect a patrician air in the attitudes to the masses, who included my immediate and extended family. Neither could I embrace the market solution and its liberal ideology. My family, particularly my paternal grandmother, taught me that capitalism meant exploitation and that when rich people spoke about individual freedoms and the national interest what they really meant was their freedoms and their interests. The golden rule of politics, I was told, is that those with the gold make the rules. The end result is a desire on my part to work towards some kind of bottom-up socialism which gives (so-called) ordinary people real rights and opportunities and a real measure of power over their own destinies without reference to an overpowerful state or total reliance on uncaring market power. This chapter is a product of that concern.

Beyond the Debate

Economic Growth and the Good Life

Up until the early eighteenth century economic practices were often subsumed under moral doctrines: there were prohibitions on usury and price-fixing was common. The Christian Church was determined, in principle if not in practice, 'to assert the superiority of moral principles over economic appetites' (Tawney, 1938, 279). By the twentieth century this conception had been reversed. A major assumption throughout the capitalist world now is that economic growth is both the means and the end of social progress. The traditional socialist challenge to capitalism seems only to question the distribution of the products of growth; it shares the belief in growth. Growth has brought benefits: people have more material possessions and there has been a degree of liberation from the constraints of previous generations. These are not to be dismissed lightly, but there have also been costs: economic growth has brought environmental degradation and alienated work experiences; a system has been created that is self-perpetuating yet unable to achieve its own explicit goals; continued expansion means continued consumption, which involves engendering continued dissatisfaction. The good life is like a carrot held out before a donkey, always visible but never attainable. Satisfaction is not your present car but the next one, the best video is not the one you are watching but the one you will buy tomorrow, and the best holiday will not be this year but next.

National achievement and performance is now measured by crude economic statistics, such as rate of growth, GNP figures and export figures. These statistics are important, but they have now taken on a talismanic quality, with the bald figures alone giving a spurious feeling of quantitative reliability. They have become a force in our lives: if the GNP figure is good, then the country is doing well; if the GNP is down, then that is bad for the country. We do need measures of economic performance but if they become the measures of well-being we are in serious trouble. We need a whole series of alternative measures of the quality of life. If Japan is the leader, with its impressive growth statistics based on strict work discipline, pressurizing conformity, overcrowding and pollution levels so high that people in Tokyo have to get fresh air from a slot machine, then we must seriously question whether we really want to be in the same race.

All countries cannot be like Japan; there are limits to growth, ecological and social. A great deal has been written about the former, and I will do no more here than repeat that much of our economic growth has been, and continues to be, based on the exploitation of finite resources. Continued economic growth has a polluting present and a shaky future. We pursue growth to the detriment of our collective health, ecological resources and long-term sustainability. Our economic-growth machine squanders the resources of the earth, despoils our collective home and blights the prospect of future generations. As Bahro (1978, 1982) and others have shown, the level of environmental pollution seems very similar on both sides of the Iron Curtain, suggesting a structural similarity between industrialized societies irrespective of the mode of production and the pattern of ownership. Oil slicks and chemical pollution, whether capitalist or socialist, American or Russian, kill birds, destroy habitats and wreck ecosystems.

There are also what Fred Hirsch (1977) has described as the 'social limits to growth'. In growth economies, more 'positional' goods are consumed; these are goods whose consumption depends on the positions of other consumers. For example, once basic housing needs have been met, people want a country cottage or a penthouse flat or whatever the current fashion dictates. The satisfaction obtained from these goods is dependent on the actions and positions of others. The rural retreat remains desirable only as long as other people do not fill up the countryside with other cottages. The penthouse is great only as long as other penthouses do not block the views. If everyone lives in a cottage in the country, no one lives in the countryside; they have merely created another suburb.

We need an alternative calculus to the present one of economic growth. We need to define individual goals and social achievements that are life-enhancing, sustainable and friendly to others and to the planet. We need a conception of economics as if people matter, which sees work for people rather than people for work and which can extend our attainable horizons beyond the dreary baseline of crude economic-growth statistics. Economic

Plate 8.1   Is this road sign in Australia telling us something about the pursuit of economic growth?

arrangements need to be reordered to fit in with our varied needs and aspirations; at present, we fit our preferences around economics. Although alternative communities exist, where people have dropped out, my preference is for dropping in and changing attitudes. Let us begin by questioning the assumption that sits, toad-like, on popular debates, that economic growth is the only criterion for the good life, the main goal of national governments, the beginning and the end-point of human interaction.

Economic Structures

In the capitalist world the growth path is maintained by powerful multinational corporations, who weave the threads of the world economy. Large capital exercises power in government and over the lives of ordinary people: markets are dominated by a handful of huge corporations; public policy is tailored to attracting and maintaining their capital investment programmes; and the very fabric of our daily life is full of the advertising slogans and artefacts of a corporate culture. To reorder our priorities and revise social goals, we need to establish alternative sources of economic power. Where corporate capitalism is providing jobs there is unlikely to be a strong demand for an alternative economy but in the black holes of contemporary capitalism, where traditional economic growth has faltered, there are greater opportunities for the creation of alternative economies. Here the national and local governments could support diverse experiments in cooperative ventures, self-help schemes and community enterprises. Such schemes may provide the basis for a human use of capital and the opportunity to create places where economic growth is not the only definition of the good life.

Jonathan Porritt (1984) has suggested that the state should maintain the formal oligopolistic economy in the short term but that the longer-term goal should be a more localized, informal economy of small-scale concerns predicated on sustainability and resource conservation. Local banks and regional enterprise boards could be established to develop local economies on the basis of local resources and knowledge. This would place local economies further beyond the whims of the international market. Porritt's argument is a step in the right direction; it fits in with my previous remarks about developing a more 'local–central' system of government. There would be a difficult transition period, of course; some areas would be better placed to achieve self-reliance than others and disputes about the goals and methods of achieving self-sufficient economies would be inevitable. It is not a blueprint for an instant utopia but the long-term prospect is an attractive one. It would reduce the power of a capitalism guided only by the pursuit of profit and there would thus be sensitivity to the limits to growth and greater responsiveness to the wishes of local communities. People would have the opportunity to build economies to suit their lives rather than structure their lives to suit the economy.

Economic Enterprises

The traditional capitalist-versus-socialist debate about industry has centred on the issue of public versus private ownership. The

Plate 8.2   An international corporate culture dominates much of our public life, as in this advertising hoarding in Austria.

left has argued for a major role for public ownership – and it has a point – but the debate about economic enterprises needs to be widened to include links between firms and employees and between firms and the local community. A more recent alternative is the 'small-is-beautiful' school, which has argued for a reduction in the size of enterprises (see Schumacher, 1973). I find this school of thought, which questions the gigantism of modern life, attractive and important, but no matter how big or small an enterprise is, real progress depends on changing the social relations of production.

Work is a central element in people's lives; it takes up much of our time and most of our energy. For the vast majority of us it is what William Morris described as 'useless toil rather than useful work'. For most of the labour-force, work is an alienating experience, which gives neither satisfaction nor much purpose beyond

Plate 8.3 The decline of traditional industries, as witnessed by the abandoned shipyard in Govan on Clydeside, Scotland (*above*), raises major problems of unemployment. Can small-scale alternatives, such as Govan Workspace Ltd (*below*) provide realistic answers?

providing a wage. The traditional socialist-versus-capitalist debate focuses too much on the level of employment. The only questions raised are: How many jobs are created? What is the level of unemployment? Our notion of employment needs to be widened, so that we consider the quality of work. If you ask people whether they would prefer to work or be unemployed, most people would prefer to work – but this is not the only question we should be asking. We must develop socially useful forms of work, which enhance the creativity and involvement of workers. Engaging the workforce should be just as important a goal as employing the workforce. To create new jobs in which people simply mind machines is, I suppose, better than nothing, but, on a scale of one to ten of encouraging individual initiative, I would rate it below one.

A strange asymmetry can be seen in much political thinking. Many writers, politicians and commentators have called for an informed and active citizenry in the sphere of public politics but say little about the workplace. A concern with involvement should not cease when people step inside the factory gate or office lobby.

Creativity and purpose are the two main requirements for work to be a rewarding experience. If people can exercise a measure of control over their work, exercising their brain as well as their brawn, then job satisfaction will be higher. Work has to have a purpose: people can recognize non-jobs and the pursuit of careers in spurious occupations leads to cynicism. The most rewarding jobs are those which give opportunities for creativity, provide a living wage and have a beneficial effect. People like to do, and like to be seen to be doing, good works. Our cities provide numerous opportunities for congenial employment, from beautifying our cities with gardens to mending footpaths and building playgrounds. Too often job-creation schemes fail. In principle they are a good idea but in practice they are used to discipline the unemployed, to make them suffer a bit. Real job-creation schemes involve the workers in the goals and strategies of the employment. Let us allow people the dignity of being involved in identifying, as well as doing, useful employment.

Empowerment means giving more power to people over public as well as private life. Engagement allows people a say in the formulation and implementation of goals across a range of

Plate 8.4   A workers' cooperative in Edinburgh, Scotland, part of a growing movement in which the quality of work, participation and collective decision-making are important elements.

activities. Full empowerment and extensive engagement should give individuals the opportunity to lead fuller working lives.

Work in the twentieth century has been dominated by an extreme division of labour. In the early part of this century F. W. Taylor, in his influential time and motion studies, showed how profits could be increased if work were reduced to a sequence of mechanical acts. The subsequent application of Taylorism in industry has maximized productivity and minimized creativity. The goal has been to squeeze out individuality and reduce work to acts capable of quick and constant repetition. There has been an effective deskilling of many crafts and trades. The end result has been that work is seen as a means to an end, not a satisfying experience in its own right.

Taylorism is not restricted to the capitalist world. Lenin was appreciative of the efficiency brought about by Taylor's methods and today work in the Soviet Union has a similar form to work in the west. Car factories in Detroit and Moscow have many similarities.

For most people, both east and west of the Iron Curtain, work is a dull, boring experience, which fails to capture their interest or use the full range of their talents; too often management represents a command relationship rather than a method of encouraging participation and creativity. While a student, I used to work on building sites in the summer holidays as a means of making money. I remember suggesting to a foreman that we move the concrete mixer closer to where the concrete was to be poured, as this would have minimized the wheelbarrow-pushing for we wheelbarrow-pushers. He looked at me and said, drawing an invisible line with his finger across his neck, 'Listen son, you are paid from here down.' His attitude is widely held, though rarely expressed in such stark terms, and reflects a concern with status. Status is important, and any assessment of human nature has to take it seriously; but we can surely devise systems of management that give people status, without denying the creativity of others. The role of managers should not be primarily to impose discipline but to engender participation and creativity. The alternatives are plain:

Either we will have a future in which human beings are reduced to a sort of bee-like behaviour, reacting to the systems and equip-

ment specified for them; or we will have a future in which masses
of people, conscious of their skills and abilities in both a political
and technical sense, decide that they are going to be the architects
of a new form of technological development which will enhance
human creativity and mean more freedom of choice and expression rather than less. The truth is, we shall have to make the
profound political decision as to whether we intend to act as
architects or behave like bees. (Cooley, 1980, 100)

The only way to engage the workforce is to transfer meaningful control to the employees, to give them power over the form
and the end-product of their labour. Employee participation that
involves a say in the means but not the ends of production
constitutes partial engagement. While not realizing the ultimate
goal, it is a useful starting-point.

The workforce can be engaged in a number of ways, from
direct ownership of enterprises and equal representation with
shareholders on the board through to decentralized work practices on the factory or office floor. We must keep the options
open, since one form may not suit all enterprises. Central and
local governments can aid engagement by making some forms of
employee participation compulsory. We already have compulsory
legislation about safety standards; employee participation should
be seen as part of a wider definition of the quality of working
life.

The state should go beyond enacting the appropriate legislation. Governments are major employers in their own right and
can develop employee participation schemes for their own workforce, thus providing a demonstration effect to private industry.
Governments also dispense money and contracts to the private
sector. Preferential treatment with contracts to firms practising
employee participation would have an important influence on
private-sector work practices.

A society that encourages and harnesses the creative power
of its citizens is a better society than one which does not; 'If a
worker is constrained through Taylorism at the point of production, it is inconceivable that he or she will develop the self-
confidence and the range of skills, abilities and talents which
make it possible to play a vigorous and creative part in society as
a whole' (Cooley, 1980, 47). The cult of the expert, rigid power
hierarchies and the stereotypical labelling of people are all signs

of a failure to use the full range of human creativity. In work practices, as elsewhere in society, we have too few systems of thought, modes of management or government initiatives that recognize the vast richness of human potential.

Community Concern

The character of contemporary capitalism, in which the viability of whole communities can be destroyed by disinvestment, suggests the need for an alternative. Even on crude accountancy terms, such drastic effects are a tremendous waste of human and physical capital – they may represent a rational decision for an individual firm perhaps, but at tremendous social costs. The traditional capitalist-versus-socialist debate says little about community imput. Kirkpatrick Sale (1980) has suggested a range of community-enterprise links that would make for better, more socially informed decision-making:

1 Community representation through contractual obligations in which firms pay over a certain percentage of their turnover to the community;
2 Community representation on local boards of management with a certain number of positions given over to directly elected members or local politicians;
3 Community ownership of assets, with workers 'renting' these for fixed periods;
4 Full community ownership and direction.

Some of these schemes will be more suited to particular societies or particular periods than others. They are not once-and-for-all-time solutions. Each has its particular difficulties. In the case of the first suggestion a number of questions arise. Should the money be paid to the local government or should separate funds be set up? The former sounds very much like a local income tax on business. Who should represent the community? And for how long? How can conflicting views within the community be resolved? There are difficulties with each of these schemes, but they represent ways in which communities can have a greater say in the nature and direction of economic activity. Enterprises have effects on local areas, they employ local labour and take up community space. We need to link workplaces with living places

Plate 8.5   Capital seeks to privatize its profits and socialize its losses; we need urban arrangements that share both costs and benefits. The slogan on the hoarding of this speculative office block in Canberra, Australia, contrasts with the 'message' of the new building.

so that neither enterprises nor local authorities can act in too irresponsible a manner.

Towards a Mixed Economy

The economic crises which have destroyed the traditional economic bases of many cities provide the opportunity for imaginative responses. The time is now ripe for experiments in community ownership and employee cooperatives. Rather than attract foot-loose capital with costly incentive schemes, which, even if successful, will probably be at the expense of some other city, we can develop feasible alternatives. Local solutions are not a substitute for national policies, they are a vital part.

If we see people as emancipators rather than as prisoners of their economic situation, then we can begin to develop schemes that build upon human resources. In the village of my birth unemployment is a common experience. There is now a flourishing people's taxi service as the unemployed with cars hire themselves out to neighbours and relatives. The drivers can afford their repayments, neighbours get a good service. This sort of ingenuity is too rarely recognized or encouraged in traditional responses to unemployment. We can imagine mixed urban economies in the fullest sense: a mix of public and private ownership, different schemes for employee engagement, the encouragement of both formal and informal economies and varying experiments in community production. We also have to consider the product of labour and encourage safer, softer products. Community production of polluting, life-threatening products is no great advance.

In the mixed economy that I envisage, the market would have an important role without being the sole criterion for measuring human welfare. We need markets. The encouragement of competition allows consumers an important say. Centralized planning, in contrast, can be inefficient, costly and dangerous, and give more power to centralized bureaucrats. Centralized economic power can lead too easily to centralized political power and ultimately to totalitarianism. Markets are important and cannot be dismissed easily by critics of capitalism. Naive socialism is as bad as crude capitalism.

We must strive to realize the advantages of a post-Fabian socialism and a post-corporate capitalism. We need truly mixed economies, which have the benefits of planning without the all-powerful bureaucrats and the efficiency of markets without the capitalists.

To create better cities we need an engaged workforce, community involvement in economic activity and a better quality of working life. To achieve these goals we require detailed strategies and particular forms of social mobilization. Above all else, in this society of casino capitalism, where private appetites are lauded and selfishness encouraged, we need a better vision of a better society. The humane city will be found,

> Not in Utopia – subterranean fields –
> Or in some selected island, Heavens knows where!
> But in the very world, which is the world
> Of all of us, – the place where, in the end
> We find our happiness, or not at all!
> (William Wordsworth, 'The Prelude', 1805)

Appendix 1
A Note to the General Reader

We can no longer identify specifically urban problems or urban issues separate from wider society. The city is not an independent unit of enquiry; it is the locale of larger economic processes and broader social issues.

Cities throughout the world are connected by economic links of trade, capital investment and disinvestment. We cannot understand the housing problems of Calcutta, the fiscal crisis of New York or the transformation of central Sydney without reference to the changing nature of the world economy. Economic changes, and in particular the restless nature of capital flows in search of profit, are registered in the towns and cities of the world. The rise of new financial centres, the demise of established ones, the growth of new industrial regions in Asia and the decline of smokestack cities in North America, Europe and Australia are all part of a general process. The growth of Osaka is linked to the decline of Detroit, Birmingham and Wollongong.

Recent years have seen a restructuring of world capitalism as production processes have shifted to cheaper labour areas, such as South-East Asia. Governments in the industrialized countries have responded in a variety of ways. Most policies have been dominated by attempts to attract and keep capital with attractive

A number of readers suggested that I incorporate these appendices into the text and dispense with them as separate entities. 'They are too specific' was the criticism. But their specific quality is important. They show, I hope, how my general arguments relate to particular audiences.

Appendix 1 is a revised version of a paper I was invited to give at the session 'Urban Development Issues of the 1980s' at the 55th Australian and New Zealand Association for the Advancement of Science (ANZAAS) Conference held at Monash University, Melbourne, 30 August 1985.

incentives and planning agreements. Capital equals jobs, so the argument goes, but this simple equation ignores questions of the quality or sustainability of employment. To attract low-paying, low-skill jobs, which may well evaporate with small-scale changes in profitability, is of no real benefit. It may be better than unemployment but it will not bring major lasting improvements to the quality of people's lives. Experience shows that cities dominated by branch–plant-type jobs do not have a secure future. Production processes change, market trends alter and profitability may dip. Footloose capital can easily move again, and cities and citizens can be back where they started.

There are alternatives. In poorer cities of the world interesting experiments with intermediate and appropriate technology have built upon the labour reserves that are available. In some richer countries, workers' cooperatives and self-help schemes have highlighted the importance of the quality as well as the quantity of employment. There is a tendency to dismiss these alternatives because, as yet, they do little to mop up the massive levels of unemployment. The argument is that global forces dominate our lives and small-scale initiatives are of little importance. That is the voice of despair, an acceptance of defeat in the struggle to control our lives and set our own priorities. We can think globally but act locally. We can begin by seeing the greatest resources of a city as its citizens, who too often are seen as the problem rather than the solution.

We have many types of language for discussing the city. Different academic disciplines even have their own dialects; hence urban geography, urban economics and urban history. In the public sphere, cities have become the arena of public administration and political compromise. Private corporations see cities as significant only within a calculus of profitability. If we want to improve our cities, then it is important to 'see' cities as if people matter. The real urban development issue of the 1980s is how to create better cities for all the citizens by providing better environments, a sense of engagement in civic life and sustainable, enjoyable employment.

Appendix 2
A Note to Academics

Recent years have witnessed an increasing use of the term 'crisis'. It has been used in a variety of contexts: the 'urban crisis', the 'fiscal crisis', the 'crisis of legitimacy' and the more encompassing 'economic crisis', to refer to the ending of the long post-war boom and rising levels of unemployment. Despite its heavy use the term has been used too narrowly. The ambivalent nature of what the term describes is captured in Chinese where the word for 'crisis' is composed of two figures: one signifies danger, the other signifies opportunity.

There are good reasons why the danger elements of crisis have been highlighted in academic debates. The effects of the economic crisis have been particularly acute in the education sector, especially in the tertiary education sector where many of us find employment. Cutbacks in education spending have seen a narrowing of job opportunities. It has been too easy for us to widen our individual experiences to greater significance. Academics in Western Europe and North America have become infected by a sense of pessimism, that pervasive feeling of unease found in all societies whose pre-eminence is no longer assured. Britain's decline, from an imperial power with an optimistic intelligentsia to a second- or third-rate power where intellectual life has a pessimistic flavour, has been the most marked. But the same trend is also evident in the USA, where the world dominance of the 1950s has been replaced by the uncertainty of the 1980s. The production, dissemination and consumption of ideas are affected by such global power shifts.

Appendix 2 is a revised version of an editorial for the journal *Environment and Planning, Series D: Society and Space*, vol. 1, 249–50, 1983.

Yet crises also create opportunities: witness the rise of important social movements for peace and women's rights. There have also been important developments in political practice. The economic crisis in Britain pushed some radical local authorities to intervene directly in local economies because of the scale of job loss and the failure of traditional policies. In the case of the now-defunct Labour-controlled Greater London Council for example, an economic policy group – informed by radical critiques, which saw traditional and industrial policies as an aid to private capital, and influenced by the demands of the labour movement – set up an enterprise board to invest in different forms of ownership and fund new cooperative ventures. Only a few local authorities have pursued such radical strategies, and the alternative job creation schemes are only a drop in the rising ocean of unemployment. However, these modest measures may represent the beginnings of a substantial shift in the direction of economic policy. The recent initiatives, although small in size and impact, are pregnant with political consequences.

We must be wary when examining such opportunities. The easiest mistake is to see the present as simply a rerun of the past. Our intellectual baggage is weighed down with past experience. In periods of unchanging development this poses no problem, but when we live in times of rapid change (and the use of the term 'crisis' is a good measure of the rate of change) our conceptual structures are often unable to explain, or even describe, new developments. We must avoid seeing new experiences through the prism of irrelevant intellectual configurations. The notion of prolonged unsustainable economic growth is no longer tenable, but neither are the prescriptions of classical Marxism. If the apologists of late capitalism have been proven wrong, then the dominant radical criticism has been equally wide of the mark. It is too easy to romanticize new movements, and to see community action, the peace movement, inner-city riots and radical local authorities all as prefigurative of a new and better society, but such phenomena have their own logic, independent of the wishes and desires of academic observers.

Let us consider afresh, the opportunities, as well as the dangers, in the present crisis.

Appendix 3
A Note to Building Workers

The dramatic turnaround in the financial picture has not been achieved easily. It has only been possible by denying worthwhile requests for increasing expenditure in areas such as education, health and welfare.

Western Australian (Labour) Premier Brian Burke on his 1984–5 Budget, which recorded an $8 million surplus.

As building workers you are faced with two major issues. The first is the question of public expenditure. This is a key element of real wages in the construction sector as well as the social wage of the wider community. Public expenditure provides one of the biggest sources of demand for building while also providing many goods and services, such as education, health and recreation, available to ordinary people on the basis of need rather than income. Yet around the world such expenditure is a source of controversy. The official policy of conservative and some not-so-conservative political groups in Europe, North America and Australia is to reduce government spending and redirect it away from welfare services.

The ideology of monetarism questions the very concept of public expenditure. With recession and the resurrection of conservative ideology, clearly expressed in Reaganomics and Thatcherism, monetarism has become an accepted part of economic policy. However, the class-based nature of monetarism needs to be highlighted. Economic ideas are not iron laws beyond the

Appendix 3 is a revised version of an invited talk to building union representatives at Clyde Cameron College, Wodonga, Australia, in August 1985.

realm of social relations and political change; they are social constructs, which aid some groups and disadvantage others. The time is ripe to launch an offensive against the prevailing ideology. The notion of economic policies pursued in the 'national interest' must be seriously questioned and the distributional consequences of government policies must be identified. We need to reveal the social consequences of monetarism that have been hidden by general slogans and the pursuit of taken-for-granted economic goals.

However, even if you are successful in shifting the debate and influencing policies that is not the end of the matter. More spending on construction and building is not your only goal. There is a second issue that must be faced: what types of city are you building?

Through negotiation and discussion you have a role to play in setting priorities. In any building programme the number of office blocks has to be balanced against the number of houses needed. Building workers need to think about such priorities if they are to be involved in pressing governments for more funding.

As building workers you have a legitimate concern with the types of building that you construct. Your working experience allows you to identify safe and unsafe dwellings, desirable and undesirable buildings, good and bad environments. Construction workers need to consider the social implications of buildings. Rather than seeing a building project as just so many jobs, you have to ask who gains and who loses; construction jobs at any price is too high a price to pay. I am asking you to consider the social consequences of your labour. Construction workers have a duty and a right to be concerned with the types of city they are building. You and your families have to live in the cities you build.

Guide to Further Reading

A number of works have been cited in the text. Here I want to provide a guide to further reading, more personal than comprehensive. I have selected those books which I have found most interesting, and grouped them under topic, not chapter, headings. Since booklists are dated from the day they appear I have also included a list of relevant journals.

Cities and Capital

Chapter 2 telescoped a number of issues. General studies that take a broader perspective are Mumford (1961) and Girourd (1985). The Victorian city and the rise of capitalism are considered by Briggs (1963), Dyos and Wolff (1973) and the immensely readable Engels (1958; originally published in 1845).

David Harvey (1973, 1987a,b) has provided the most sustained analysis of the relationship between capitalism and urbanization. Others worth considering are Badcock (1984) and Dear and Scott (1981). Peter Hall (1981) gives a lively account of Kondratieff cycles. Alternative forms of investment form part of a radical rethinking of our economic and social structure; for good guides to this literature see Fromm (1976), Schumacher (1973), Henderson (1981) and Porritt (1984). Various schemes with local ethical investment include, in the UK, the West Midlands Enterprise Board and the Greater London Enterprise Board. In the USA there is the Self Help Association for Regional Economy based in Barrington, Massachusetts. See the journal *Local Economy*.

Journals that treat the broad theme of cities and capital include

International Journal of Urban and Regional Research, Environment and Planning, Series D: Society and Space, Capital and Class and *Marxism Today.*

Cities and community action

Manuel Castells was a leading light in the Marxist-inspired writing on the city in the 1970s and early 1980s. In his *City and the Grassroots* (Castells, 1983) he undertakes a cross-cultural study of community action. For studies of the USA see Piven and Cloward (1977). Gibson (1979), Leonard (1975) and O'Malley (1977) provide UK examples. Gibson (1984) shows how professionals can help neighbourhoods to control their own environment and future. There are also the journals *Community Action, Grassroots, Community Development* and *Community Care.*

Cities and Design Professionals

A delicious introduction to architecture is given in cartoon form by Osbert Lancaster (1975). Wolfe (1982) castigates the rise of modernism, Jencks (1987) surveys its replacement by postmodernism and Knevitt and Wates (1987) examine more participatory forms of architecture. Amongst the many journals in this field, the following are worth browsing through: *Architectural Design, RIBA Journal, Architectural Review* and *The Architect's Journal.*

Peter Hall (1988) gives a grand tour of the history of urban planning. National planning histories include Cherry (1981), Streeton (1970), Scott (1969) and Krueckenberg (1983). International connections and comparisons are discussed in Sutcliffe (1981). On a contemporary note, Peter Ambrose (1986) asks what happened to planning and Goodman (1972) aims a general broadside attack. Gans (1968) is very readable. Amongst the planning journals see *Town Planning Review, Planning, Environment and Planning B: Planning and Design, Journal of the American Planning Association, Environment and Planning A.* On the effect of design on behaviour see *Architecture and Behaviour* and *Environment and Behaviour.* The Town and Country Planning

Association has maintained its utopian heritage and its journal is a great source of information on participatory planning and alternative plans, and in general provides a point of sustained commitment to the idea and practice of creating better, fairer, more beautiful cities.

Cities and the Future

People have been thinking about future cities ever since the first group met at the first tavern to moan about the existing order. Todd and Wheeler (1978) cast a backward look at the utopian tradition. Baynes (1987) looks to the future of cities with a regard to design innovations. A range of journals, both specific (e.g. *Alternatives, Futures* and *Social Inventions*) and more general (e.g. *Built Environment, Urban Studies, Environment and Planning* (*Series A, B, C* and *D*), *Urban Affairs Quarterly, Cities, International Journal of Urban and Regional Research* and *New Society*) will give you a fair selection of material to consider the urban future. Remember you have a role to play – it's your future too.

Cities and Life-cycles

People's needs, aspirations and skills vary over their life-cycle. Academic studies of the cycle from different sociological and psychological perspectives include Berger and Berger (1976) and Berg and Boguslaw (1985).

On children see Ward (1978), Michelson et al. (1979) and Kopp and Krakow (1982). On late childhood/early adulthood see Brake (1980) and Goodman (1960). Erikson (1978) gives an introduction to the adult years. The range of relevant journals includes: *Child Development, Youth and Society, Family Process, Human Development* and *Urban Education*.

The greying of our attitudes is a recent phenomenon, but now there are a host of studies concerned with the social aspects of ageing. Any of the following are worth looking at: Rowles and Ohta (1983), Blau (1981), Fontana (1977) and issues of *Journal of Gerontology* and *The Gerontologist*.

Cities and Politics

In chapter 6 the most important individual authors have been cited, so I will just note here a few other interesting readings. Peter Self (1985) provides a comprehensive review of political theories of government, while Held et al. (1983) and BBC (1984) provide general introductions to the history of political thought. Bernard Crick (1962) gives a spirited defence of politics against both enemies and friends. An anarchist position is developed by Michael Taylor (1982), while Walzer (1970, 1983) and Nozick (1974) slug it out from positions that, in terms of public-service provision in the city, may be described as left and right, respectively. The relationship between political ideology and urban politics and planning is at the heart of Peter Steinberger's (1985) discussion. Boddy and Fudge (1984) discuss the local–central theme. Levi and Litwin (1986) and Lisk (1985) deal with the problems and practices of popular participation. Most of the political science journals are, to use someone else's quote, devices for avoiding politics without obtaining science. A rare exception is the *Political Quarterly*. You will be better informed if you read good newspapers and weeklies. *New Statesman & Society* and *The Economist* cover the political spectrum with readable and lively reporting.

Cities and Traffic

The most readable account of urban transport issues that I have come across is Thomson (1977). Other interesting studies include Adams (1981), Tyme (1978) and Schaeffer and Scalar (1975). For journals see *Transportation Research, Transportation, Transportation Quarterly* and *Traffic Quarterly*.

Cities and Welfare

An iconoclastic view of education and medicine is given by Illich (1971, 1976). With reference to housing, see the general studies of Birchall (1988), Ward (1985) and Ospina (1987). Ballantyne (1988) and Hatchett (1987) provide case studies of participatory and public housing, while Ball (1986) takes on the reform of owner-occupation. Hackney (1988) gives an architect's argument for consultation in the building of social housing, Marcus and Sarkission (1986) provide detailed guidelines. For journals see *Roof* and *Social Work Today, New Society, Municipal and Public Services Journal, Social Work, Public Administration Review, Social Policy* and *Journal of Social Issues.*

Cities and Women

There is now an important and lively feminist critique of urban structures. For a range see Wekerle et al. (1980), Matrix (1984) and McDowell (1983). Hayden (1981) provides a historical study of feminist designs for the city. *Signs,* especially the special supplement to volume 5, *Women in the American Cities* (Spring 1980) and *Spare Rib* are just two feminist journals worth examining. Watson (1986a,b) concentrates specifically on the important issue of access to housing. See also *Gender and Society.*

Cities and Work

In 1885 William Morris made the distinction between useful work and useless toil. His views are still worth reading; see the volume edited by Briggs (1984) as an introduction to this influential writer. The influence is clear in Robertson (1981), Cooley (1980) and Roszak (1981). General reviews of new forms of work and technology include Shakin (1986) and Noble (1986). On self-management see Vanek (1975) and Thornley (1980). On urban unemployment see Hasluck (1987). Alex Nove (1983) provides a compelling account of the economics of feasible socialism, which combines both planning directives and market forces. See also *Work and Occupations* and *Economic and Industrial Democracy.*

Green Cities

I have said very little about the actual physical design of cities. This is deliberate. Appropriate, humane designs arise most often,

I believe, when there is a blend of full discussion, community participation and expert knowledge all allied to a concern with straddling that difficult balance between historical connectivity and forward progress. However, there are some basic design questions that I think are self-evident. The referencing of nature in our urban spaces cannot be overestimated. We have a need for contact with grass and plants and the appropriate facets of the living world. On the greening of cities see Nicholson-Lord (1987). Nan Fairbrother (1972) presents a readable account of landscape design and Jackson (1984) is at his polemical best. *Landscape Architecture, Landscape Design* and *Landscape* are interesting journals.

Bibliography

Adams, J. G. U. (1981) *Transport Planning: Vision and Practice*, Routledge & Kegan Paul, London.

Alinsky, S. (1969) *Reveille for Radicals*, Vintage, New York.

Alinsky, S. (1972) *Rules for Radicals*, Vintage, New York.

Ambrose, P. (1986) *Whatever Happened to Planning*, Methuen, London.

Axelrod, R. (1984) *The Evolution of Cooperation*, Basic Books, New York.

Badcock, B. (1984) *Unfairly Structured Cities*, Basil Blackwell, Oxford.

Bahro, R. (1978) *The Alternative in Eastern Europe*, New Left Books, London.

Bahro, R. (1982) *Socialism and Survival*, Heretic Books, London.

Ball, M. (1986) *Home-ownership: A Suitable Case for Reform*, Shelter, London.

Ballantyne, A. (1988) When design is the real criminal. *Guardian*, 9 March, p. 23.

Banham, R. (1971) *Los Angeles: The Architecture of Four Ecologies*, Allen Lane, London.

Baynes, K. (1987) *Cities With A Future*, Channel 4 Television/ Design Council, London.

BBC (1984) *Political Thought from Plato To Nato*, BBC, London.

Berger, P. L. and Berger, B. (1976) *Sociology: A Biographical Approach*, Penguin, Harmondsworth.

Berg, W. M. and Boguslaw, R. (1985) *Communication and Community: An Approach to Social Psychology*, Prentice-Hall, Englewood Cliffs, NJ.

Birchall, J. (1988) *Building Communities*, Routledge, London.

Blau, Z. S. (1981) *Ageing in a Changing Society*, Franklin Watts, New York.

Boddy, M. and Fudge, C. (eds) (1984) *Local Socialism*, Macmillan, London.

Brake, M. (1980) *The Sociology of Youth and Youth Subcultures*, Routledge & Kegan Paul, London.

Briggs, A. (1963) *Victorian Cities*, Odhams, London.

Briggs, A. (ed.) (1984) *News from Nowhere and Selected Writings and Designs*, Penguin, Harmondsworth.

Castells, M. (1983) *City and the Grassroots*, Edward Arnold, London.

Cherry, G. (1974) *The Evolution of British Town Planning*, Leonard Hill, Leighton Buzzard.

Cherry, G. E. (ed.) (1981) *Pioneers in British Planning*, The Architectural Press, London.

Christensen, T. (1981) The politics of redevelopment. In D. T. Herbert and R. J. Johnson (eds) *Geography and the Urban Environment*, John Wiley, London.

Cooley, M. (1980) *Architect or Bee*, Langley Technical Services, Slough, Berks.

Crick, B. (1962) *In Defence of Politics*, Weidenfeld & Nicholson, London.

Davie, M. (1983) The great flat roof disaster, *Observer*, 11 September, p. 40.

Dear, M. and Scott, A. J. (eds) (1981) *Urbanization and Urban Planning in Capitalist Society*, Methuen, London.

Dworkin, R. (1977) *Taking Rights Seriously*, Duckworth, London.

Dyos, H. J. and Wolff, M. (1973) (eds) *The Victorian City: Images and Realities*, 2 vols, Routledge & Kegan Paul, London.

Engels, F. (1958 edn; first published 1845) *The Condition of the Working Class in England in 1844*, Basil Blackwell, London.

Erikson, E. H. (ed.) (1978) *Adulthood*, W. W. Norton, New York.

Fairbrother, N. (1972) *New Lives, New Landscapes*, Penguin, Harmondsworth.

Fontana, A. (1977) *The Last Frontier: The Social Meaning of Growing Old*, Sage, Beverly Hills, California.

Friedman, M. and Friedman, R. (1980) *Free to Choose*, Secker & Warburg, London.

Fromm, E. (1976) *To Have or To Be*, Jonathan Cape, London.

Galbraith, K. (1958) *The Affluent Society*, Hamish Hamilton, London.

Gans, M. (1968) *People and Plans*, Basic Books, New York.

Gibson, T. (1979) *People Power: Community and Work Groups in Action*, Penguin, Harmondsworth.

Gibson, T. (1984) *Counterweight: The Neighbourhood Option*, Russell Press/Town and Country Planning Association, Nottingham.

Girourd, M. (1985) *Cities and People*, Yale University Press, New Haven and London.

Goodman, P. (1972) *After the Planners*, Penguin, Harmondsworth.

Goodman, P. (1960) *Growing Up Absurd: Problems of Youth in the Organized System*, Random House, New York.

Hackney, R. (1988) The people's choice, *Guardian*, 29 February, p. 36.

Hall, P. (1981) The geography of the fifth Kondratieff cycle, *New Society*, March, pp. 535–57.

Hall, P. (1988) *Cities of Tomorrow*, Basil Blackwell, Oxford.

Harvey, D. (1973; reissued 1988) *Social Justice and the City*, Basil Blackwell, Oxford.

Harvey, D. (1987a) *Consciousness and the Urban Experience*, Basil Blackwell, Oxford.

Harvey, D. (1987b) *The Urbanization of Capital*, Basil Blackwell, Oxford.

Hasluck, C. (1987) *Dealing With Urban Unemployment*, Longman, London.

Hatchett, W. (1987) Thamesmead: the new model town, *New Society*, 20 November, pp. 9–10.

Hayden, D. (1981) *The Grand Domestic Revolution: A History of Feminist Designs for American Homes: Neighbourhoods and Cities*, MIT Press, Cambridge, Mass.

Hayek, F. A. (1982) *Law, Legislation and Liberty*, Routledge & Kegan Paul, London.

Held, D., Anderson, J., Gieben, B., Hall, S., Harris, L., Lewis, P., Parker, N. and Turok, B. (1983) *States and Societies*, Martin Robertson, Oxford.

Henderson, H. (1981) *The Politics of the Solar Age*, Anchor/ Doubleday, New York.

Hillman, M., Henderson, I. and Whalley, D. (1976) *Transport Realities and Planning Policy*, Broadsheet 567, Political and Economic Planning, London.

Hirsch, F. (1977) *Social Limits to Growth*, Routledge & Kegan Paul, London.

Illich, I. (1971) *Deschooling Society*, Calder & Boyars, London.

—— (1976) *Limits to Medicine*, Marion Boyars, London.

Jackson, J. B. (1984) *Discovering the Vernacular Landscape*, Yale University Press, New Haven, Conn.

Jencks, C. (1987) *Postmodernism*, Academy Editions, London.

Kendig, H. L. (1984) *Contributions of the elderly*, Proceedings of 19th Annual Conference, 94–7, Australian Association of Gerontology.

Knevitt, C. and Wates, N. (1987) *Community Architecture*, Penguin, Harmondsworth.

Kopp, C. B. and Krakow, J. B. (1982) *The Child: Development in a Social Context*, Addison-Wesley, Reading, Mass.

Krueckenberg, D. A. (ed.) (1983) *The American Planner: Biographies and Recollections*, Methuen, New York and London.

Lancaster, O. (1975) *A Cartoon History of Architecture*, John Murray, London.

Le Corbusier (1927) *Towards a New Architecture*, John Rodker, London. (First published in French in 1924 as *Vers une Nouvelle Architecture*, Editions Crés, Paris.)

Le Grand, J. (1982) *The Strategy of Inequality*, Allen & Unwin, London.

Leonard, P. (ed.) (1975) *The Sociology of Community Action*, Sociological Review Monograph 21.

Levi, Y. and Litwin, H. (eds) (1986) *Community and Cooperatives in Participatory Development*, Gower, Aldershot, Hants.

Lisk, F. (1985) *Popular Participation in Planning*, Gower, Aldershot, Hants.

McDowell, L. (1983) Towards an understanding of the gender division of urban space. *Environment and Planning, Series D: Society and Space* 1, 59–72.

Macpherson, C. B. (1962) *The Political Theory of Possessive Individualism*, Oxford University Press, Oxford.

Marcus, C. C. and Sarkission, W. (1986) *Housing as if People Mattered: Site Guidelines for Medium-Density Family Housing*, University of California Press, Berkeley and Los Angeles.

Matrix (1984) *Making Space: Women and the Man-made Environment*, Pluto Press, London.

Michelson, W., Levine, S. V. and Spina, A. (eds) (1979) *The Child in the City*, 2 vols, University of Toronto Press, Toronto.

Mumford, L. (1961) *The City in History*, Secker & Warburg, London.

Mumford, L. (1968) *The Urban Prospect*, Harvest/HJB, New York.

Newman, O. (1973) *Defensible Space: People and Design in the Violent City*, Architectural Press, London.

Nicholson-Lord, D. (1987) *The Greening of the Cities*, Routledge & Kegan Paul, London.

Noble, D. (ed.) (1986) *The Forces of Production*, Alfred A. Knopf, New York.

Nove, A. (1983) *The Economics of Feasible Socialism*, Allen & Unwin, London.

Nozick, R. (1974) *Anarchy: State and Utopia*, Basic Books, New York.

O'Malley, J. (1977) *The Politics of Community Action*, Spokesman Books, Nottingham.

Ospina, J. (1987) *Housing Ourselves*, Hilary Shipman, London.

Packard, V. (1961) *The Waste Makers*, Penguin, Harmondsworth.

Paul, J. (1981) *Reading Nozick*, Basil Blackwell, Oxford.

Piven, F. F. and Cloward, R. A. (1977) *Poor People's Movements: Why they Succeed, How they Fail*, Pantheon, New York.

Porritt, J. (1984) *Seeing Green*, Basil Blackwell, Oxford.

Rawls, J. (1971) *A Theory of Justice*, Belnap Press of the Harvard University Press, Cambridge, Mass.

Rees, I. B. (1971) *Government by Community*, Charles Knight, London.

Robertson, J. (1981) *The Redistribution of Work*, Turning Point, Ironbridge, Shropshire.

Roszak, T. (1981) *Person/Planet*, Granada, St Albans, Herts.

Rowles, G. D. and Ohta, R. J. (eds) (1983) *Ageing and Milieu*, Academic Press, New York.

Sale, K. (1980) *Human Scale*, Coward, McCann & Geoghegan, New York.

Sayle, A. (1984) *Train to Hell*, Methuen, London.

Scarman Report (1981) *The Brixton Disorders, April 10th–12th 1981*, Cmnd 8427, HMSO, London.

Schaeffer, K. M. and Scalar, E. (1975) *Access for All: Transportation and Urban Growth*, Penguin, Harmondsworth.

Schumacher, E. F. (1973) *Small is Beautiful: A Study of Economics as if People Mattered*, Blond & Briggs, London.

Scott, M. (1969) *American City Planning Since 1890*, University of California Press, Berkeley and Los Angeles.

Self, P. (1985) *Political Theories of Modern Government*, Allen & Unwin, London.

Sennett, R. (1970) *The Uses of Disorder*, Alfred A. Knopf, New York.

Shakin, A. (1986) *Work Transformed*, Holt, Rinehart & Winston, New York.

Steinberger, P. J. (1985) *Ideology and Urban Crisis*, State University of New York Press, Albany.

Streeton, H. (1970) *Ideas for Australian Cities*, Georgian House, Adelaide.

Sutcliffe, A. (1981) *Towards the Planned City: Germany; Britain; the United States and France 1780–1914*, Basil Blackwell, Oxford.

Tawney, R. H. (1938; first published 1926) *Religion and the Rise of Capitalism*, Penguin, Harmondsworth.

Taylor, M. (1982) *Community, Anarchy and Liberty*, Cambridge University Press, Cambridge.

Thomson, J. M. (1977) *Great Cities and their Traffic*, Victor Gollancz, London.

Thornley, J. (1980) *Workers' Co-operatives: Jobs and Dreams*, Heinemann, London.

Todd, I. and Wheeler, M. (1978) *Utopia*, Orbis, London.

Tyme, J. (1978) *Motorways versus Democracy*, Macmillan, London.

Vanek, J. (ed.) (1975) *Self-Management*, Penguin, Harmondsworth.

Walzer, M. (1970) *Obligations*, Harvard University Press, Cambridge, Mass.

Walzer, M. (1983) *Spheres of Justice*, Basic Books, New York.

Ward C. (1978) *The Child in the City*, Architectural Press, London.

Ward, C. (1985) *When We Build Again Let's Have Housing that Works*, Pluto, London.

Watson, S. (1986a) Women and housing or feminist housing analysis. *Housing Studies*, 1, 1–10.

Watson, C. (1986b) *Housing and Homelessness: A Feminist Perspective*, Routledge & Kegan Paul, London.

Wekerle, G., Peterson, R. and Morley, D. (1980) *New Space For Women*, Greenwood, Westport, Conn.

Wolfe, T. (1982) *From Bauhaus to Our House*, Jonathan Cape, London.

Index

Index by Ann Barham